The Moral Debate on Special Education

COUNTERPOINTS

Studies in the Postmodern Theory of Education

Shirley R. Steinberg
General Editor

Vol. 444

The Counterpoints series is part of the Peter Lang Education list.
Every volume is peer reviewed and meets
the highest quality standards for content and production.

PETER LANG
New York • Washington, D.C./Baltimore • Bern
Frankfurt • Berlin • Brussels • Vienna • Oxford

Bernardo E. Pohl, Jr.

The Moral Debate on Special Education

PETER LANG
New York • Washington, D.C./Baltimore • Bern
Frankfurt • Berlin • Brussels • Vienna • Oxford

Library of Congress Cataloging-in-Publication Data

Pohl, Bernardo E.
The moral debate on special education / Bernardo E. Pohl.
p. cm. — (Counterpoints: studies in the postmodern theory of education; 444)
Includes bibliographical references.
1. Special education—Moral and ethical aspects. I. Title.
LC3969.P65 371.9—dc23 2012032458
ISBN 978-1-4331-2108-1 (hardcover)
ISBN 978-1-4331-2107-4 (paperback)
ISBN 978-1-4539-0950-8 (e-book)
ISSN 1058-1634

Bibliographic information published by **Die Deutsche Nationalbibliothek**.
Die Deutsche Nationalbibliothek lists this publication in the "Deutsche Nationalbibliografie"; detailed bibliographic data is available on the Internet at http://dnb.d-nb.de/.

The paper in this book meets the guidelines for permanence and durability of the Committee on Production Guidelines for Book Longevity of the Council of Library Resources.

29 Broadway, 18th floor, New York, NY 10006
www.peterlang.com

Printed in the United States of America

To my parents, Monica and Bernardo, and my siblings, Maria, Cintia, and Freddy, who taught me that no dream is impossible, helped me to be who I am today, and never took an excuse or a no for an answer.

In loving memory of:

Joe. L Kincheloe

and

Ernestina de Torrecilla

Gone but never forgotten. May their legacy live forever.

ACKNOWLEDGMENTS

One of the greatest myths of our society is the concept of "individual achievement." No such thing exists. No one person produces a book by his or her own, just as no person can pull herself or himself up by his or her own bootstraps.

It is, of course, impossible to fully acknowledge all of those who have helped and supported me in this journey, as family, friends, colleagues, and students have always supplied me with their enthusiasm, encouragement, ideas, and criticism. I will always be grateful for having my mentor, teacher, and dear friend Dr. Cameron White—who encouraged me with his energy, genius, and passion for social justice in education. This is definitely not a project that I could have ever started and completed without his guidance and support. There are other doctoral colleagues and co-workers who have been instrumental in this journey-Cheryl Craig, Susan McCormack, the late Sabrina Marsh, Yali Zou, Jason Apodaca, Judy Owens, Neil Liss, Jacob Newman, Debbie Shulsky, Dustine Thomas, Randy Seevers, Chris Witschonke, John McKay, Cheryl Cook, Nancy Hartsfield, and Sam Brower are among them.

I will always be indebted to Michelle Harrold and Dr. Chloe Diepenbrock at the writing center at University of Houston-Clear Lake. They graciously came aboard at the eleventh hour and helped me with the titanic task of properly learn how to write, proofread, and finish a book. It is because of them that this book is a reality. Otherwise, I would still be talking about the "book" that "I am writing."

I will always be grateful for the mentorship, friendship, and guidance of Shirley Steinberg and the late Joe L. Kincheloe. They believed in me, when I just a graduate student, always trusting that my writing was worthy of publishing. Thank you for being so real and genuine to so many of us and not just the printed words.

Most importantly, I will always appreciate the patience and dedication to this project by Chris Myers and everyone else at Peter Lang Publishing. They never backed away—always believing that this project would become a book, sooner or later. The rest of you know who you are, and I will thank you, when the time comes.

TABLE OF CONTENTS

ONE

THE MORAL DEBATE

How can I forget? Everyone stared at the department chairperson in amazement. Our jaws simply dropped. In seconds, the room was a mixture of unrest, anger, and disbelief. It was not that we had not seen this coming. After all, she had warned us for months that "changes were coming from above." However, this was just another rock hitting us from behind, which caught us off guard. Yet to each of us in that room, it was clear that we were not winning our struggles to make special education meaningful for our students. At least, I did not see it that way. Instead, policies and regulations would take precedence over the well-being of the student (Cremin, 1983). Again, we relegate the learning experience of the disabled students over the standard demands of productivity and result. The concerns for making a meaningful learning experience for the disabled were not considered.

It was hard to bring order to the room, but emotions slowly got under control long enough to hear the new changes that the Legislature and the Texas Education Agency were considering. They decided that taking state-mandated tests was the best for all students in special education—from kindergarten to twelfth grade. In two years, all special education students, except in the most extreme of cases, would have to take some form of the state-mandated assessment called TAKS (Texas Assessment of Knowledge and Skills). From then on, all special education curricula would have to be integrated with the mainstream for the "benefit" of standardized testing (Hehir, 2005).

As I began working on this project five years ago, the question proposed by holistic educator Ron Miller (1990/1997) kept resonating in my mind: What are schools for? And in the same manner, I ask: What is special education for? The images these questions provide are the driving force and backbone behind this piece of work. For behind our society's ups and downs in the current cultural turmoil in education, we cannot ignore and avoid the lasting social, political, and economical effects that education vests upon our lives.

The Personal and Theoretical

This is a multilayered project. First, it has a broader (telescopic) argument trying to make sense of the current crisis and turmoil in the educational arena at large (R. Miller, 1990/1997; Purpel & McLaurin, 2004). On one hand, we are constantly expecting better performance and better results from students, which means making the education environment resemble the workplace more and more (Apple, 1995; Giroux, 2003a). However, parents and interest groups, such as the media, political activists, and corporate leaders, are also demanding better school performance (R. Miller, 1990/1997). The result from these demands is total social confusion about what we want out of education and from our public schools. Society demands that schools should be the places where students are educated and become productive members of society, but we are constantly at odds in how to achieve it.

As a society, we no longer question the quality of education that is given to our students, the appalling conditions of our schools, the second-class treatment of our teachers, or the non-rigorous and visibly mediocre learning standards needed to pass a standardized state-mandated test. As Purpel (1989) points out, America's great faith in education does not match our actions. Furthermore, Cremin (1983) argues that public education is ignoring society's most pressing needs. The result is an educational system investing great amounts of energy in knowledge mastery, but indifferent to the most important social issues of our time (Cremin, 1983).

Another layer of this work is the microscopic argument. It explores how the current educational crisis is also part of special education. Beyond the argument of whether inclusion and special education work or not (Erevelles, 2000; Gabel, 2002; Hehir, 2005), it is my position that the field is also engulfed in utter confusion. How do the demands of better performance and results influence special education? What will happen when the scores of disabled students are incorporated into the standardized testing craze? My biggest question is: Did we really erase the barriers or simply create new ones?

Finally, this is a scholarly and theoretical work. It examines the problems that I have with special education, analyzing the hope that I find in critical pedagogy and moral education. These narratives, along with its contradictions, ambiguities, and promises, are part of my life experiences, which I intend to represent by placing my personal life within a theoretical context (Ellis, 2004).

The Journey

This is an academic journey. It was in the academy that I have experienced the biggest revelations about the political, social, cultural, and economic aspects of public education. It was in these halls of the academy, by the hand, and with the guidance of Cameron White, Neil Liss, Jason Apodaca, Susan McCormack, Sabrina Marsh, and many others, where the initial passion for social justice in education was put in me with their examples and where my passion to raise my voice and demand a better place for the disabled was unleashed. It was in the sanctity of the ivory tower and the hallways of the academy where I heard the initial roar telling us "we can do better" for the students and for education, and this is a roar that has not left me.

This is also a personal journey. It cannot be any other way. It is personal because I have to face my innermost demons about education, disability, and my life. I realized that no journey is more important than the journey upon which I have now embarked. This is a journey without airports, trains, or passports, but this is a spiritual journey into the innermost corners of my soul, facing the teacher, the immigrant, and most especially, the disabled within me.

The Debate We Need

I have several reasons for doing this project. The first reason is that the twenty-first century is offering us, as a society, the opportunity to re-conceptualize our cultural, political, and social position as a nation and as human beings like never before. Recent world developments, such as the possible resurgence of the Cold War, the threat of terrorism, the current threat of genocide, famine in the Third World, the current financial debacles, and irreversible ecological disasters, should be warning bells to all of us that things are not business as usual.

In the wake of these challenges mentioned above, the second reason for this project is that I do not find a serious educational discourse in which the core purpose of special education is being thoroughly examined from the outside of the current dominating and restricting social framework. The latest waves of educational reforms, which were designed to rethink the practice as a whole, have only contributed to the dreariness and bleakness of the profession. What has truly emerged from the latest reforms is a series of top-down policies that continue to sustain the century-old rigid traditional hierarchy of education. In this system, we continue to see teachers treated as mere technocrats, students as recipients of information, and the public-at-large as ignorant individuals of the educational policy-making process. The latest educational reforms in special education have come with a serious lack of imagination, when it comes to rethinking our schools' purposes.

I am undertaking this task with a firm belief that the fields of disability, especially in academia, have ignored crucial calls for a serious moral debate in education. For all the promises and successes once envisioned by educational reforms for the disabled, we are seeing the profession being reduced to psychometrics, numerical standards, and testing performance. The typical case is that if the numbers are good, then everything is fine. In the same light with David Purpel (1989), I am convinced that the disability movement of the 70s, in the same light of the civil and radical movements of the 60s, did not seriously challenge the existing social, political, and cultural structures of the time; rather, it was pleased with certain accommodations and structural changes within the existing social framework. Serious calls to redefine the social constructions of disability in a more humane light were never made. Furthermore, it is safe to argue that contrary to racial discrimination, which often sparks serious social outrage, discrimination against the disabled does not. Furthermore, it might be even safe to say that it continues to enjoy a certain degree of social acceptance (Ferri & Connor, 2005).

I see serious implications in the minor organizational changes that emerged from the 60s and 70s civil right movements, which mostly did not challenge this nation's core cultural values. We, as a society, can find an example of this in our public schools. At the end of the first decade of the twenty-first century, very little has changed in the way we operate and manage our schools. We continue to have the same model adopted in the wake of the American Industrial Revolution, demanding discipline, rigid school structures, and an enormous emphasis on classroom management (Urban & Wagoner, 2000; Zinn, 2003). Hence, most of public schools in this nation are becoming dreadful places for the average student, where the same thing is taught year after year. From previous decades, very little has changed in the way the four basic core subjects, English, mathematics, natural sciences, and social studies, are taught. Vibrant schools and invigorating classrooms are increasingly becoming the national exception, instead of the norm.

The Urgency

Special education, for decades, has not been part of the larger educational debate. In many ways, it has been left in the margins, constructing it owns universe, with the medical side at one end and the social side at the other. Advocates on the medical side see disability as a dysfunction within the body in need of correction, and the ones on the social side see disability as the social construction of barriers. However, we seldom see special education as a realm of the larger context of general education, and we rarely believe that it might, actually, be facing the same crises encountered by the rest of public education.

America has a great amount of faith in education. There are two things that we, as a society, hardly disagree on. First, that education is the foundation of the great democratic experiment of this nation. Second, that the economy is one of the central institutions of our nation. We seldom argue about what we expect out of public schools, which is preparing citizens for their civic duties and the workforce. We rarely disagree that schools are places where we can send our youth to learn English, math, history, football, art, and cheerleading. We take for granted that schools are places where the young learn about love, hate, sexuality, life, friendship, rivalry, and death. America has created an institution like no other in the world. At any given town, city, or neighborhood, public schools in America are at the center of the community in ways and forms that we cannot witness anywhere else in the world.

As I said, we disagree very little on the fact that public schools are the foundation of our democracy, and that society, as a whole, has vested a great amount of faith in the educational system of this country. Yet, such faith has been met with very little support in terms of resources for students and teachers. The working conditions for educators continue to be appalling, offering very little rewards and professional growth. Students continue to attend school for six to seven hours a day, with very little flexibility in what they can do and learn. Unfortunately, these appalling conditions multiply themselves exponentially in the special education field.

It is not clear yet why society has accepted these abysmal standards for public education. One clue, given to us by Purpel (1989), is society's lack of awareness, self-deception, and avoidance of a profound moral discourse in education. However, the most uncomfortable possibility is society's distrust and suspicion of the intellectual process, given that it is not a mystery to anyone that America has a tradition of anti-intellectualism and a love affair with the applied, the technical, and the practical. In the end, Americans simply accept passively that politicians, journalists, and the industrial establishment can attack an institution that actually worked very effectively for generations, until the Reagan administration started to attack public schools with the publication of the *Nation at Risk* in 1983 (Berliner & Biddle, 1995). As a result, we, as a society, seldom strive to provide a better learning environment, rarely question the motives of the establishment attacking our public schools, and never raise our voice demanding better from public officials. Somewhere along the line, the general public accepts a working and learning environment with strict guidelines and rules, very little opportunity for changes, and a serious lack of ingenuity in terms of what can be done.

TWO

A NOTE ON MY JOURNEY

I still remember the day very well. I was sitting in class when I was called to the office. The secretary tells me to sit and wait. I waited for about an hour until I am told to go into an office. At that time, I was confused. When I went into the office, I saw some familiar adults who were part of my life such as my Dad, my counselor, a teacher, and the therapist. In that meeting, they told me that I was going to have some schedule changes and some new services. The meeting with me lasted for ten minutes or less, and then, I was dismissed.

Over the years, these meetings would become a battleground. In there, I would argue that I hated my classes, and that I wanted to take drafting and be an architect. Over and over, I was told that it was too hard for me, to be realistic about my future and college, and that they have better classes more suitable for me. In the end, it was always their decision and not mine. And in the end, my wish did not matter. They knew better.

During my years as a high school student, I did not have a clue what those meetings were about. I never knew that I even had some IEPs. It was not until I became a teacher that I realized what an ARD meeting was. During my entire high school years, I was kept in the dark, forced to accept what I was told, and survive in a world that did not work for me.

I decided to do this project because of the serious questions that I have about what public education is today, which has not changed significantly from previous years. Education in our public schools is not measuring up to what we would like it to be. I believe that the question is not how resources or funds need to be allocated in the schools. Instead, we need to start asking ourselves why we have accepted such low standards for education to the point where people can be kept in the dark about their future, especially for the disabled students. We should be wondering what conditions would truly provide an excellent educational experience for teachers and students.

This project originated from my interest in justice and equality in education, especially for the disabled. As I began to look for factors of equality and justice, I came to two conclusions. One, that the fields of disability and special education have avoided more contentious questions regarding the treatment of disabled students. It is undeniable that some people see the inclusion of the disabled as a triumph. However, what are the implications of placing so many disabled students in the general education classrooms and with the same deficient standardized curriculum that is taught to the general student population? The second conclusion is that any meaningful change in special education will require us to seriously ponder about the nature and the quality of special education. Changes that simply restructure the existing rigid social arrangements to accommodate the disabled will not be enough. What is needed is a complete reframing of our cultural awareness of the disabled, which continues to look at the disabled as unable individuals. For example, instead of always coming up with the same old excuses that "they can't do it" or "this is not for them," it will require us to come up with avenues to make the disabled successful in academically demanding settings.

A Note on Structure

In this book, I include a literature review and my theoretical foundation, so I can outline in larger-grained detail the telescopic argument. I intend to review the work of those scholars in critical and holistic pedagogy that influenced my moral view of general and special education. Furthermore, I intend to review the current scholarly work in the field of disability studies, examining how that relates to the moral/social justice aspect of education. My argument is that society has avoided fundamental moral questions regarding education and disability. As in the rest of education, the moral debate of special education continues to be limited to technical questions regarding the implementation of curriculum, inclusion, assessment, and IEPs to name a few. Society continues to avoid a deeper and more meaningful discussion of a larger vision of what special education could be.

I will also outline my research methodology: narrative inquiry, which has helped me unleash my inner voice. I borrow from Clandinin and Connelly (1992) that teachers are not curriculum dispensers but curriculum makers. As such, and over time, the curriculum becomes the lived experiences of teachers and students (Aoki, 1989/1990; Clandinin & Connelly, 1992; Craig, 2006b). As a special educator, I will explore the possibility of the special education teacher as a curriculum maker rather than a mere knowledge dispenser.

My Journey as a Narrative

In the last part of the book, I intend to unleash my narrative, which analyzes my story, providing the context that makes my vision for a pedagogy for the disabled more understandable. I hope to propose an intimate and detailed look into my own life as a disabled and non-disabled individual. Although I believe that my life is by no means peculiar, I do believe that the experiences of my life encountered certain sets of events that fundamentally shaped my view of disability. Without a doubt, it has deeply influenced my personal perspective on teaching. It will be the moral reflection of my teaching experience, providing an intimate window on my view on life, which has deeply influenced my teaching practice. In these chapters, I plan to give an intimate account of my life as a special education teacher.

Along with my narrative, I will envision the pedagogy for the disabled. It will build from all previous chapters, and I intend to discuss the possibilities of liberating pedagogy for the disabled. Questions regarding liberation, oppression, and conscientization for the disabled will always surface. People in favor of and against such possibilities will always flood our academic journals and bookshelves. We will always be puzzled by what can constitute a liberatory pedagogy for the disabled.

Why did I decide on narrative self-inquiry? According to Jerome Bruner, narrative can allow us to formulate a better version of "ourselves in the world" and provide better ways to create "identity and agency" (quoted in Craig, 2006b, p. 263). According to Bruner (1991), it is through narrative that we can best develop a world of reality.

Furthermore, as Bruner (1996) explains, narrative is a hermeneutical process in which we can create meaning.

This research is a hermeneutical process, which analyzes how different agencies shaped my identity. I want, as well, to explore the agencies and the identity that created meaning in my life. By using Craig's (2006) validation of the teacher's voice, I want to place the teacher as an integral part of special education and its possible outcomes. In this context, I am fully aware that the teacher of special education is an integral part of the educational environment. The fact that I am also a disabled individual adds an extra variable to the equation. Therefore, this becomes a unique case where there are not only special education students, but also there is a disabled teacher.

The teacher in the unfolding story is myself. I am not only a teacher in special education, but I am somebody who received special services as a student in secondary school. Originally, the intent was to retell my story as a special education teacher from day one to the present. As my career evolved, however, it became evident that my experience as a teacher was different from my experience as a special education student two decades ago. As a teacher, I became entrenched in the politics and interests shaping the special education curriculum, which I believe are not that different from the rest of the educational field. As my research and interests developed, the idea to offer a chronological event of my first four or five years as a special education teacher evolved into using my narrative as a medium to understand special education within the larger moral context of education.

There is no doubt that over the years this project has become a highly personal endeavor. By using narrative as personal tool, I can foster the narrowing of the gap between the academic, the practical, and the very personal. At the same time, I can allow myself to explore my inner knowledge and my own voice. Like the rest in the fields of narrative and social justice, I am one of many who is fighting for equality and justice, making no claim that I have discovered the answer to deal with the many tensions and dilemmas that exist in special education. My narrative, like many narratives in disability studies that precede me (M. Carr, 1995; Gabel, 2002; Hehir, 2005; Reiser, 2006a; Valentine, 2007), only seeks to unmask the indigenous knowledge of my unique position in the field. Semali and Kincheloe define indigenous knowledge as:

> an everyday rationalization that rewards individuals who live in a given locality. In part, to these individuals, indigenous knowledge reflects the dynamic way in which the residents of an area have come to understand themselves in relationship to their natural environment. (quoted in Valentine, 2007, p. 129)

My narrative seeks to understand the dynamic in which I have come to see myself—where I can reflect about my life as a doctoral researcher, a teacher, an immigrant, a disabled individual, and a former special education student during secondary school. I use narrative to organize my knowledge and my beliefs as a disabled teacher in special education, as well as how I have come to terms with my environment and my indigenous knowledge. This is what Connelly, Clandinin, and He (1997) refer to as personal practical knowledge, which is defined as the overall teacher's "personal experience" involving all aspects of his or her life (p. 666).

I would tend to believe that the most potent moral question today for anyone involved in special education is to wonder if it is really working or not. After three decades, I think we should be asking whether Public Law 94–142 (The Education of All Handicapped Children Act; PL 94–142 hereafter) achieved what we wanted it to achieve. Perhaps we should be wondering if we truly want inclusion within the current deficient standardized frameworks of general education, or if we can envision something totally different and radical for our time and for the disabled. However, I assume that these are powerful questions if one is to take these questions seriously, knowing well that education does have serious consequences in our life.

I always wanted to be an architect. During high school, I badly wanted to take drafting, but nobody wanted me. Remember those annual meetings? I always argued to be enrolled in drafting, and I was always discouraged from enrolling in those classes. The argument was that theses classes were too hard for me, and that they did not want to see me fail. Seven years later, I earned an architecture degree. In retrospect, I assume there was more to the story. It is my assumption, as argued by Valentine (2007), that questions regarding the true validity of special education need to be put into a larger context in terms of how the classroom, the school, and the overall educational experience impact a student's life. It will be better if we can focus more on the long-term effects rather than on the immediate results of data and testing for the sake of students' performance. However, if I were to address this in terms of the larger context of politics, economics, culture, society, bureaucracy, and performance of teachers and students, I am afraid that we would not be seeing the field of special education working very well.

One of the biggest dilemmas that I see in special education is what the initial intent of PL 94–142 was, and what it has become. Originally, it was meant to serve children with severe disabilities as Valentine (2007) argues. However, as Bursztyn points out:

> Most children served in special educationare not those with severe needs, but rather those with mild behavior and learning problems who are difficult to differentiate from those not designated as disabled. (quoted in Valentine, 2007, p. 130)

Within this context, I believe that my narrative developed out of several concerns that I have about special education. One of my biggest concerns is in regards to the official professional knowledge currently governing education today. For example, let us take testing/evaluation as a problem in our public schools. Initially developed to help the teachers and facilitators make concise decisions about the proper services and accommodations for a child with special needs, the field is littered with jargon, vagueness, and psychometrics, which are impossible to understand unless one is indoctrinated in deciphering the code (Valentine, 2007). Even if teachers receive the proper training to decipher and analyze these codes, we need to question the validity of the proper diagnosis if, as Valentine (2007) argues, results are already outdated only months after a diagnostician performs an evaluation. It should not surprise us that schools perform testing and evaluation for legal ramifications that suit the districts, administrators, and legal advocates fairly well; sadly, and for the most part, the question about how to properly create a desirable learning environment continues to be unanswered to this day (Purpel & McLaurin, 2004). It would be safe for us to assume that this is also the case for the disabled, given that politics and policies regulate so much about what happens in special education.

In that regard, I am trapped in a big dilemma because my first reaction is that special education is not working if what we want is to provide is a meaningful educational experience for the disabled. Furthermore, my temptation is to go as far as to say that we are positioning ourselves for failure. If anything, it is out of luck that special education continues to sustain itself as an institution, considering the chaos that is engulfing the practice. However, it is during this time that memories of what we have done and what works in special education start to emerge. These are the images of my close relationships with parents, students, and other teachers in a profession in which we struggle together to accomplish the very best each day in the life of the disabled.

This helps restore my faith in the field. However, this does not by any means assuage the extraordinary problems facing special education (e.g., teacher burnout, lack of resources, angry parents, inadequate placement, bureaucratization, inclusion, and assessment). At first glance, I realize that it is easier to focus on the problems than on the solutions. I also realize that it has not been very easy for people to extend the problems that we find in general education into special education. However, special education needs a critical examination that will foster change, which radically challenges the field.

In the end, I see the need to explore a pedagogy for self-reflection that helps us reinvigorate ourselves in a process that must empower students and teachers. With that in mind, I offer my narrative, my experience, my voice, and my own personal history in special education to those entering the profession of education for the first time and to those already in the trenches, as a mode to promote a more critical discourse in special education.

We still have many groups that continue to be marginalized in our society, and their voices and needs continue to be ignored. This is an educator response to the current situation of special education. This book is an attempt to argue that special education cannot longer ignore the gate-keeping forces that shape the general education field. We do a great disservice to our students if we continue to believe that general education and special education are two distinct entities which are shaped by different needs, philosophies, and ideals, because nothing can be further from the truth. If anything, special education traditionally serves as the first laboratory where administrators experiment with staff reduction, budget cuts, mandated curricula, and classroom size increases. This research arises from my belief that the special education students will also encounter the same social upheavals, tribulations, tensions, and uncertainties that the rest of the student population encounters. They are also the victims of the same neoliberal curriculum and economic forces of injustice and inequality.

THREE

WHEN SCHOOLS DON'T WORK

> When I give food to the poor, they call me a saint. When I ask why they are poor, they call me a communist.
>
> —Brazilian Archbishop Dom Helmer Camara

The bell rings, and the day starts like any other. It is first period, my conference hour, so I go downstairs, check my mailbox, and run some copies. On my way to the teacher's lounge, I stop by the coffee pot to fix my first cup of coffee. As the hour progresses, I start getting the daily feeling of a heavy stone setting in my stomach. Ten or fifteen minutes before second period, anxiety creeps in my body and time becomes a slow motion movie in anticipation of the second period mayhem.

So, who will be doing what today? Will Mark come with his arms full of freshly inked satanic tattoos? Will he curse me when I tell him to go wash it off his arms? Will Emily slam the door shut in purpose to scare me one more time? Will Rick sit on the floor angry in a corner, putting his hoody over his head because Pete called him a faggot again? Will Steph say over and over how much she hates this f***ing class throughout the 45 minute period? Well, none of that happened that particular morning.

By the time class started, however, the anxiety, fear, and anticipation were too much to bear. And on that day, the mayhem came from me.

It was ten or fifteen minutes into second period, and I could not take it anymore. Unable to teach for five minutes without someone misbehaving, I was becoming increasingly frustrated. In the middle of class, on that morning, I grabbed my backpack and left, leaving behind the students with the class aide. It was then when I got to know Jake (not his real name).

Jake was one of my students in my math class. He was 21. Convicted of a crime for which he did hard time, he went back to high school to finish his senior year. This was his last year. I was literally opening my car door when, from behind, Jake slammed it shut. He asked me what I was doing and if I was crazy.

He said, "Dude . . . come back! . . . teachers don't leave class!"

I told Jake, "I don't want to do this S**** anymore. I can't take it!"

He begged me to come back, and I did. I told the class that it was a free period for the rest of the hour, and I put a movie on the VCR. I told the aide to keep an eye on the kids, and I sat with Jake in the hallway outside my classroom. It was then that Jake told me his story, and I told him mine. I learned that he was blamed for bringing pot into the school, and that even though his innocence was proved in court, the judge still sent him to juvenile, so that he could learn "a lesson" about hanging out with the wrong crowd. I told him that I never wanted to be a teacher in the first place. I told him that I messed up in architecture school, that I graduated with mediocre grades and a bad portfolio—teaching was what was left for me to do.

Jake told me that he never spoke to a teacher the way he spoke to me. After that day, and for a week and a half, I would sit with each of my students in the hallway, and I would listen to what they had to say and learn who they were. My experience with Jake is not unique. Over the years, I have made an effort to know my students personally, as I remember that the teachers who influenced my life the most were those who were interested in knowing the person inside of me. They were important to me because they made the effort to know who I was. As the year went by, Jake needed help, and he would stay with me for tutoring every afternoon. We developed a good rapport. A second time repeat of resource math, he passed my class, at the end of the year, on his own effort.

When I decided to become a teacher, I had the conviction and belief of making my practice a transcendental experience. I was already involved in the doctoral program of Social Education at the University of Houston. Contrary to many teachers who become teachers first and graduate students later, I became a graduate student first and a teacher later. By the time I entered the classroom, therefore, my notions of what the classroom should be, what students must experience, and what learning must encompass were well-groomed in critical pedagogy—a philosophy of education based on praxis and social justice (Freire, 2000; McLaren & Farahmandpur, 2005). My convictions were founded on the notion that what mattered was to make sense of the world to my students in term of politics, society, and culture (Kincheloe, 2004). Like many new teachers, I went into the field with high hopes, big dreams, and the firm belief that education should be a preparation for life rather than "the transmission of authorized knowledge" (Miller, 1997, p. 220). As a new teacher, I was convinced that learning cannot happen, unless it is an action of discovery, exploration, curiosity, and a personal encounter with what matters most in life.

In the beginning, I was a teacher full of energy. I had the desire to make my classroom a constructivist-learning environment, and my classroom was going to be where students were going to discover on their own the wonders of life. As time passed, I lost the energy that I originally had. The excitement of the first weeks disappeared, and it was gone. Days became a dreadful exercise of trying to fulfill required daily tasks of accomplishing my lessons. The daily grind, stress, and routine took away the goal of making the classroom something special. Over the years, the energy, convictions, and desire reappeared, but this only happened, however, after a serious evaluation of what I wanted to do and where I wanted to go, as a teacher and individual.

In my life, I do not subscribe to a nostalgic view of school, when teachers were revered figures of vision and respected individuals of society. I do not seek some romantic vision of the world where society recognizes that education is a vital activity for our society. But, at some point, in my early days as a teacher, I did have that nostalgic view. That is because somewhere in my youth, I did encounter those revered teachers, and somewhere in my school days as a student, education was a vital activity in my life; my teachers were people with visions. I was taught that education was important in my life, that it would have serious consequences, and that I was to take it seriously (Purpel, 1989). Nevertheless, as a teacher, education for me ceased to be important as the days went by. I was taking it seriously, but for the wrong reasons, and I did not care about the serious consequences that education would yield.

All of that would change during the Christmas of 2004. I headed for Denver. I longed to see my newborn nephew and my family that I had not seen for a while. One afternoon, when everyone went Christmas shopping, I decided to head for a coffee shop and read a book that a doctoral colleague recommended to me. I needed something new and fresh to read. By that time, I was unable to go beyond page one with Freire's *Pedagogy of the Oppressed* (1970) or Dewey's Democracy and Education (1916/1944)—books that are pillars of my doctoral foundation. One afternoon, I opened David Purpel's *The Moral and Spiritual Crisis in Education* (1989). From the start, this was a refreshiing journey into uncharted waters, which I needed. What was missing? I was missing the poetic message that, honestly, I believe critical pedagogy lacks at times. We, critical pedagogues, are not known for our poetic language, and David Purpel was providing me with the poetic language of social justice that I needed.

Critical Pedagogy

During my student teaching, I made many people upset in my foster school. My mentor was the typical rebel without a cause. They needed him to go north; he headed south. Therefore, when he told me to skip the in-service professional development day and worry about my fifteen-page paper, I knew that I was going to be in hot water. However, the next day, the joke around the department was that I missed the gifts. As I learned, the in-service day was a textbook adoption conference—a true showcase of free books, door prizes, and free food. Publishers put on the show. And from what I heard, it was a true Hollywood-style event, along with all the bells and whistles that comes with it. It was the first time that I saw public education as a big business with bigger and more powerful interests at hand.

In my early doctoral years, the notion of researching the disabled was not on my radar screen. In those years, as a doctoral student, my influences were education and social justice, and my interest was to bridge the equality gap in the classroom. As I started to read and research, it became clear to me that American education was in a big moral dilemma. Miller (1997) asks: what are schools for? His question is a moral provocation for the current ongoing conflicts in the public school system. It is an analytical quest, exploring the purpose of education and school in the American culture. His question is a response to the dilemmas of the American school with disgruntled parents and taxpayers demanding better results in public education. The result of this is transforming the schools into prey to different interest groups, which are trying to impose their own agendas. Miller's question put in me a set of emotions, and I started wrestled with what the public-at-large expects of education, which is better performing schools. However, my biggest dilemma was to see how little these expectations equate into concrete actions that demand a better learning environment.

As a graduate student, I became a fervent advocate that teachers should help students interpret their own lived world. I adhered to the notion that school should be a meaningful place for students (Aoki, 1989/1990; Greene, 2003). As Dewey (1897) argued in his essay *My Pedagogic Creed*, schools must represent the life of the child and what that life represents to the child. In the beginning, I did not know how to create a classroom that reflected the life of the child. I knew, in my heart, that I had questions regarding the purpose of school at an academic level. I had serious conflicts about the endless demands that schools should prepare the students for the workforce from government officials, executives, and journalists (R. Miller, 1997). I also strongly disagreed, and I continue to do so, with the constant demands of state-mandated tests. After the summer that I read Miller's book, the question of what school is for became more intense for me.

In the fall of 2003, I entered the doctoral program of Social Education at the University of Houston. Unsure of what I wanted to do, and which road I wanted to pursue, I started to read whatever landed in my hands. My first book was McLaren's (2003b) *Life in Schools: An Introduction to Critical Pedagogy in the Foundations of Education*. From the start, McLaren's denunciation of capitalism and the influence of the market models on education greatly influenced me. I began to view capitalism as the economic exploitation of the masses and the product of neo-liberalism. As McLaren puts it, neo-liberalism is "capitalism with the gloves off" or "socialism for the rich"

(McLaren, 2003b, p. 22). McLaren argues that this economic model means:

> . . . . a corporate domination of society that supports state enforcement of unregulated market, engages in the oppression of nonmarket forces and anti-market policies, guts free public services, eliminates social subsidies, offers limitless concessions to transnational corporations, enthrones a neomercantilist public policy agenda, establishes the market as the patron of educational reform, and permits private interests to control most of social life in the pursuit of profits for the few. . . . (McLaren, 2003b, p. 22)

In the beginning, this single paragraph became a revelation for me, greatly influencing my frame of reference. In McLaren's view, capitalism is the erosion of social welfare and the common good for the people. It is the establishment of policies which safeguard the wealth and the privileged few. This means the total private ownership of life and the "private sector involvement in welfare and other state services" (McLaren, 2003b, p. 22). The involvement of the private sector in every part of life means the total decay of the social aspect of life. For me, however, the decay of the social aspect of life has consequences that are far more serious. It means, for me, the destruction of social goods for the sake of privation. As Giroux (2003a) argues, market-driven societies create identities shaped by consumerism; suddenly, the notion of democracy means the ability to purchase and acquire wealth. Furthermore, schools cease to be the "cornerstone of democracy" as it caters to the "ever-aggressive corporate culture" (Giroux, 2003a, p. 120). Education becomes less a force for the social good and the public welfare and more the breeding ground for future consumers.

In my early days as a doctoral student, McLaren took me by storm. He truly became an important influence in my life. My vision of education shifted. Education was not just a means to implement knowledge. It became the avenue to understand the articulation of social, political, and economical forces of society (McLaren, 2003c). I started to view education as the means for capital production, providing valuable goods for the economy, and I started to see the field as a sub-servant of the private sector, as the call for standardized testing, vouchers for private schools, and financial incentives for well-performing schools became louder (McLaren, 2003b, p. 23). Education, for me, became the first place for labor-consumer-oriented production. The CNN and Discovery Channel logos in the history books, the Pepsi-Cola machines in the football house, the science labs donated by Exxon or Shell, and the nutrition classes with lesson plans provided by McDonalds are visible intrusions of corporations in the classroom. For the first time, I could no longer see schools as mere academic centers, but as places where kids were CNNized, Pepsidized, and McDonaldized for the welfare of the rich and powerful. How can we explain, then, the fact that every ten years publishers spend millions of dollars on lunches, trips, and other perks during textbook adoption?

When Schools Don't Work

"So, where did you go? Where've you been?" I asked.
Jose looked at me and shrugs his shoulders.
"Around," he said
I looked at him, not knowing what to say. Something in me said that this was just not working for Jose.
"Around the neighborhood?" I asked again.
"Yep," he replied.
"What can I do?" I asked him, wondering if there was anything I could do. He just looked at me, pressing and biting his lips against his teeth.

Even before I started my doctoral dissertation, I knew that schools were not working. Schools don't work when students skip classes, when special education students are kept in the dark about the process, and when a teacher decides to walk away from work in the middle of the day. Schools definitely don't work when you still have students attending at the age of 21.

On the day that I walked away from my class, I did it because school was not working for any of us. It was not working for the students, and it was not working for me. This is not to say that school does not work. I believe that all institutions work for somebody, but I don't believe that schools are working for great numbers of teachers and students. Obviously, people will disagree with me. After all, millions of students graduate from our schools and go on to live productive lives. We do graduate the best students who attend the best universities in the world. And contrary to popular myth, we do rank amongst the best in academics (Berliner & Biddle, 1995). Our schools do produce some of the brightest minds on the planet. For every story of success, however, there are many more stories of failures and broken promises. At this stage of the game, this is not something we can afford to have.

FOUR

THE SOCIAL EDUCATOR

There is very little I take for granted these days. I really care about my job, and I really value what I have and what I earn. However, there was a time in my life when I took everything for granted. Life was sweet. My family dined in the best restaurants, and we took vacations in style, big time. Abruptly, everything changed back in the 80s, when the oil industry went down the drain. My Dad was lucky, and he was not fired. In order to save his job, he agreed to almost a 60 percent pay cut in his salary. Suddenly, your life changes forever. Overnight, we went from a family that could afford a Mercedes Benz without blinking an eye to a family that needed to make the hardest of choices on a daily basis, such as paying the electric or the water bill and not buying an extra gallon of milk for the week. As newcomers in the United States, we did not know the system, so we just survived on our own in the best way we could. When Dad could not give us any lunch money, Mom woke up at 3 A.M. to bake bread. Mom figured out that it was cheaper to bake our own bread. For two years, baked bread with a thin slice of ham with butter was our lunch.

This was not the first time we faced hardship. When we lived in Argentina in the 70s, Dad left for a year to work in Venezuela. After a month or so, mom stopped receiving dad's paychecks from the oil company. They told my Mom that Dad quit and took off without notice for Europe. Obviously, in the days before emails, texts, and cell phones, this was hard to corroborate. The truth was that the comptroller from the oil company in Argentina started to steal my dad's paychecks. By the time this was discovered, Mom went for months without getting any money from Dad. The result was that the rent, bills, and school tuition went unpaid.

However, there was a big difference between the crisis that my family weathered in the 80s and the one from the 70s. In Argentina, there was always somebody to help. The landlord agreed to wait for

Dad to return. My Godmother helped my Mom buy the food for us. My aunt helped my Mom as well. Yes, we went through really hard times, when Dad was away, but there was always a hand to help. In the U.S., we found ourselves dealing with our hardship by ourselves. There was nobody to run to for help. If we lost the house, we lost the house. If the water or light went unpaid, the water or light went unpaid and it was cut off. Suddenly, this was happening to us. If there was no money for lunch, there was no lunch. It was not a movie or the prime time soap. It was not somebody else's problem. This was not happening to the family three houses down the block. This time, it was happening to us. This was our reality.

Poverty and hardship for me has always been personal. In part, it was because of what my family went through in the 80s. When I was in architecture school, it was hard for me to understand the urban decay of the inner cities. This was portrayed, in the classroom, as a fuzzy image of bad governmental policies, corporate greed, social apathy, and adoration for the suburban life. Suddenly, the concept of this decay was crystallized; however, when I entered the doctoral program, urban decay was another victim of the vicious avarice of capitalism.

As I progressed in the doctoral program, capitalism, for me, was not a mere trendy economic term, which relates to the favoritism of private enterprise over public institutions. Capitalism became a term associated with "exploitation, accumulation, endless growth, and class conflict" (McLaren & Farahmandpur, 2005, p. 162). Beyond the corporate brand of intrusion in the schools, I realized that the problem was more serious. For me, this meant the total de-politization of the masses (McLaren & Farahmandpur, 2005). In other words, we, as a society, ceased to question the disparate gap in salaries between workers and executives, the erosion of job securities and benefits, the creation of entire sectors of permanent unemployment or sub-employment, and the disappearance of social welfare as a legitimate safety net in times of crisis. In the end, schools are no longer the place where we are rearing critical citizens equipped for social and civic duty; instead, we are rearing automatons ready to survive in the cruel world of capitalism, where the concept of democracy equals insatiable consumerism (Apple, 1995; Giroux, 2003a).

As a new doctoral student, I needed a foundation that would help me understand the social inequalities in North America's market economy, and I needed to see for myself the relation between education and the corporate forces (Apple, 2005; Giroux, 2003a). For the first time, it became clear to me that American schools and the corporate world were intimately connected (Apple, 1995; Apple, Kenway, & Singh, 2005; McLaren, 1980; McLaren & Farahmandpur, 2005). For example, Apple (1995) narrates that in Wisconsin the legislature demanded employment courses to become part of the curriculum at the primary, secondary, and college levels. Corporate America was demanding more servants from our schools, and the legislature, at least in Wisconsin, was listening. I, for the first time, could not view education in public schools as a place with higher social and civic learning purposes, but I started to view it as a preparation for the workforce.

My biggest revelation, however, was my understanding of the devastating effects of capitalism. Purpel and McLaurin (2004) argue that capitalism means the total erosion of the social welfare system. Capitalism creates "unnecessary individual suffering" with the privatization of healthcare and the end of unemployment benefits (Purpel & McLaurin, 2004, p. 184). Therefore, I started to view capitalism as a trap that encloses a certain sector of the population into a vicious cycle of poverty, debt, and consumerism, leaving very little safety when things happen to go wrong.

What became clear to me was that society became morally incapable of dealing with the most pressing issues of our time (Counts, 1932, 1949). What happens when the sole purpose of schools is to train students for the workplace? What transpires when entire sectors of society are left to their despair and suffering without any real relief? What occurs when society no longer cares to deal with the consequences of having so many disenfranchised? These were only a few of the questions that started to emerge in my mind.

Finding a Path

Despite my exposure to heavy doses of reading in critical pedagogy (Anyon, 2005; Darder, Baltodano, & Torres, 2003; Giroux, 1988, 2003a; Greene, 2003; McLaren, 2003a), I continued to be unsure of what to do and where to go. My academic advisor, from the beginning, told me to think about researching Latinos, disabled, and/or English learners. Although his suggestions made perfect sense, I tried to follow a different path. I wrote about anything and everything. Whether it was resistance or mere disconnection, my advisor's suggestion did not click inside of me. However, destiny had its own bag of tricks.

In the spring of 2002, I obtained my teaching certificate in Secondary History. However, because I was not an athletic coach or certified to teach other areas of social studies, finding a job as a history teacher became next to impossible. As a result, I decided to keep substitute teaching while going to graduate school. My reputation as a good 'sub' secured me daily assignments at a high school in Northwest Houston. The administration of that school was aware that I was looking for a permanent teaching position, so they kept an eye on me. After two years of not being successful in finding a permanent teaching job, I desisted from that goal. Instead, I started to contemplate other avenues where I could enhance my graduate studies, e.g., teaching at a junior college or finding an administrative job at a university.

During a lunch break at my summer job in 2004, the phone rang, and the impossible became a reality. The principal at the high school, where I substituted, offered me a part-time job as a special education teacher. I did not have a certificate to teach special education. However, I was certified to teach history, which allowed the district to hire me on a one-year emergency permit to teach special education. I had one year to obtain a permanent teaching license in special education, which I did. I also obtained a certificate to teach English as a Second Language. Overnight, I went from being un-hirable to be highly marketable. Like my mentor once said, "You just secured yourself a job for the next forty years." Nevertheless, job security was not what I was seeking. I was searching for that crucial connection that would make my doctorate studies meaningful; I thought a teaching job would give me that connection. Influenced by McLaren, Freire, Kincheloe, and other visionaries of a liberating pedagogy, I wanted to be an educator that would emancipate my students. My goal was to bring into the classroom the much-needed social consciousness that other doctoral colleagues of mine were doing. I wanted to follow their example. I wanted to be like them.

During the academic year of 2004–2005, I simply kept on writing and reading. I decided to explore what really made me tick as a doctoral student. I had moments when I was unable to write one single line, followed by moments when I would literally write forty pages in a fifteen-hour span over a single weekend. In April of 2005, I went to Montreal to attend an education conference for the first time. Hyper-charged and incredibly inspired by the education conference that I just attended, I wrote wildly for an entire week. Despite having these hyper-charged inspirational moments, I was still unable to find my destiny. I was teaching special education, working with disabled students, and attending doctoral seminars. Nevertheless, I was still unable to find a path. I became interested in philosophy, and for a moment, I wanted to pursue that direction. However, I realized that philosophy was not my passion.

Ever since I became a doctoral student, critical pedagogy has greatly influenced me. In April of 2006, I went to San Francisco for a conference. I had the opportunity to talk with critical theorists Joe Kincheloe and Peter McLaren, who are known for promoting social justice, empowerment, and equality. Empowerment for Kincheloe (2004) means allowing students to have a voice, especially those at the margin of society. This can only be accomplished when we remove the "[d]ominant powers" of school (Kincheloe, 2004, p. 9). Kincheloe's calls for serious social consciousness for empowerment greatly influenced me, and immediately, I felt the need to critically question our current state of affairs in our society. This meant, for the first time, empowering the disabled student. McLaren has also greatly influenced me, and his compelling denunciation of social and economical inequalities in urban schools has become a pivotal frame of reference (McLaren, 2003b; McLaren & Farahmandpur, 2005).

When I told Joe L. Kincheloe that I wanted to develop a critical pedagogy for the disabled, his eyes lit up like two candles. He agreed with me that the disabled student also needed to be empowered. What started as a two-minute goal to catch an autograph from Peter McLaren ended in a thirty-minute conversation. Peter McLaren agreed with me that if there was a group suffering the inequalities of capitalism, it was the disabled. Kincheloe and McLaren were supportive and told me to pursue the project. After speaking with them, my fate was sealed, and I started to pursue what I considered the Pedagogy for the Disabled, building on Freire's theme of Pedagogy of the Oppressed (1970/2000).

The Social Educator in Me

I was trying to open a bottle of tempera paint in my kindergarten class one day. I opened the cap so fast that the paint spilled all over my new uniform. The consequences of ruining my new uniform terrified me. I was worried about what would happen to me at home. I knew that my mom would be upset; after all, she had bought the uniform the day before, and it was ruined. As the event unfolded, I was overwhelmed in disbelief. The classroom became silent. Everyone became speechless. My kindergarten teacher, assuming control of the situation, took a wet cloth and tried to clean the paint off my uniform in the best way she could. Nevertheless, and after the initial shock, things returned to normal. I continued working and playing with the paint. I started to mix the paint splattered on the table, and I began to see an array of colors like a rainbow. I also continued with my original assignment, which was to use primary colors to make secondary colors.

This is one of many incidents when accidents just happened in school because of my disability; however, people around me looked at it as the normal unfolding of my life. For many years, school for me was a place for wonder and exploration; learning just happened in the form of a game. In the early years, school for me was a true playground for discovery. As I remember the day I climbed my first tree, I realized that my disability was not a limitation, a barrier, or an issue in my early school days. My disability was not an impediment. Like any other child, I was allowed to explore my world freely without constraints. In the end, I believe the manner in which I grew up greatly influenced the way that I would see myself over the years, which is as a capable human being. My ability to see myself as capable would also influence, over the years, the way I would perceive teaching millions of disabled.

As I became aware of the capitalistic forces of education, it was obvious that education had become social for me. This meant shifting from the pedagogy of the "interrogation" of the text to the "lived experiences of the students" (McLaren, 2003c, p. 170), which is something expressed by many scholars in the field since the 80s and 90s (Aoki, 1989/1990; McLaren, 1980). The call is, therefore, to understand how humans experience the world (Connelly & Clandinin, 1990). Society assumes that education is the preparation of the student for future living. Somehow, we cling to the notion and the hope of preparing our students for a distant future. McLaren (2003c), like Dewey (1897), asserts the notion that education must represent the present life. At the basics, this is a call for the lived pedagogy, which is an evolving organism in the multi-faceted environment of the classroom. This is the pedagogy that is "lived in the streets" (McLaren, 2003c, p. 170). Education, often reduced to the task of learning, memorizing, and repeating, evolved for me into a complex institution with a rich multicultural texture.

So, how did this new vision of education, as a social endeavor, look for me? After reading McLaren, I searched for other critical pedagogues that would influence me. Over the years, Joe Kincheloe's work became a major influence. As he notes:

> Educators walk minefields of educational contradictions in the contemporary pedagogical landscape. On some levels teachers and students discover that schools pursue democratic goals and education for a democratic society. . . . (Kincheloe, 2004, p. 1)

On one hand, schools must be the pillars and the backbone of a democratic society. However, it was clear to me that it was simply not enough to teach the simple mechanics of citizenry, such as knowing the Pledge of Allegiance and the meaning of voting. To me, it became obvious that such acts are merely another shallow act of citizenry (Giroux, 2003b). Social education, as I started to see it, was more than creating students that knew how to sing the National Anthem. So, how does education as the backbone of democracy look for me?

Going back to the in-service day. Very few people know the big business of the textbook industry. Moreover, very few people know that Texas and California set the standard for the textbook publishers. The rest of the country simply follows. So, when textbook adoption day approaches, it is a given that big money will be spent by publishers, luring teachers and districts to choose their textbook editions.

With the passing of time, social education meant the awareness of the different forces shaping the school setting, and at least for me, the complexity of the educational arena. Perhaps nobody can articulate better this complexity than David Purpel. On one end, there is no discussion or argument that schools are the main foundation for our democratic ideals (Kincheloe, 2004; Purpel, 1989). There seems to be little disagreement that, at the core, public education will safeguard our basic sets of democratic values, and this is where we vest great amounts of faith (Purpel & McLaurin, 2004). Nevertheless, such visions of democracy and faith in education contradict the reality in our schools. As Kincheloe points out:

> . . . on other levels they [teachers and students] find that schools are authoritarian and pursue antidemocratic goals of social control for particular groups and individuals. Sometimes participants learn that schools are grounded on cooperative values; in high-stakes driven curricula they find that a competitive ethic is dominant. (Kincheloe, 2004, p. 1)

For me, becoming a social educator was more than learning a creative pedagogical technique. It was the realization that, often, schools have mechanisms in place that do not serve our democratic ideals well (R. Miller, 1990/1997). It became clear to me from the many ARD meetings that I had to attend, as a teacher and student, during my high school years. This means that often "school knowledge comes primarily from dominant cultural, class, and gender groups" (Kincheloe, 2004, p. 1). Furthermore, as Purpel (2004) argues, the public no longer questions the appalling standards of education that are grounded in an anti-intellectual tradition. The result is a social confusion or trivialization of what we want our schools to be. As Purpel argues:

> When I speak of trivialization, I refer to two major phenomena of educational discourse—the evasion or neglect of larger more critical topics and the stress put on technical rather than on social, political, and moral issues. (Purpel & McLaurin, 2004, p. 19)

Therefore, becoming a social educator meant that I must become critical about what education was becoming. For me, education was becoming a dangerous place. By this, I mean that we, as a society, no longer promote an education that deals with the most pressing and urgent themes of our times: hunger, war, famine, unemployment, or terrorism. By "dangerous," I also mean that education is a "technical enterprise" (Purpel & McLaurin, 2004, p. 18). As Purpel points out:

> . . . in the context of both enormous problems and incredible intellectual ferment, what constitutes the focus of mainstream educational concern? Apparently, such issues as closer evaluation of teachers and students (e.g., merit pay, competence tests, periodic testing) school prayers, "middle schools," computers in the classroom, "creationism" vs. evolution, and public aid to private schools. (Purpel & McLaurin, 2004, p. 19)

It is clear that the conditions of education are appalling. After all, we only need to turn on the television set to learn about the latest attack in public education in terms of budget cuts, contracts termination, and school closures. As a society, we demand that our schools educate our children. We expect schools to be safe places where we can send them to learn. However, public education is crumbling in front of our eyes. For Purpel (1989), society no longer questions the profound and challenging questions regarding the state of education, avoiding the serious investment of truly trying to figure out the quality of education in our classroom. Rather, it seems easier to focus and channel our energies to more shallow propositions that represent testing, performance, and productivity. The consequence is the avoidance of fundamental questions regarding the cultural and social aspect of education, and the result is the lack of using education for an intense inquiry into the social and cultural state of our time. Nevertheless, we must ask why this challenge and effort has not been undertaken. Perhaps, as Purpel (2004) argues, this would constitute questioning our most basic cultural and social beliefs about this nation and our society. It would mean questioning our basic assumptions about the goals and purposes of education, and it is very doubtful that our society would like to be engaged in such a titanic effort. However, this is what social education means to me.

It is clear that critical pedagogy and moral education awoke the social educator in me. It meant seriously pondering the current state of education, which lead me to question the "ameliorating" responses to education (Purpel & McLaurin, 2004, p. 19). These are responses that do not take into consideration the most pressing and urgent issues of our time, and they are based on technocratic curricular practice. Becoming a social educator also meant becoming aware that education is in dire need of drastic changes. These drastic changes will only occur when our responses, as a society, will deal with more profound questions about society, the corporate intrusion of schools, and the unbending authoritarian hierarchy.

Social education is a "cultural/social critique" (Purpel & McLaurin, 2004, p. 19). As such, this critique requires us to fundamentally re-conceptualize the schooling process. Social education means the questioning of the current state of affairs of public schools. Perhaps, most importantly, it means asking and wondering what kind of education we want for our students. Without a doubt, asking these kinds of questions would propose contentious challenges to education. However, it would also stimulate us to consider whether or not we have what it takes to seek a humane curriculum of love, compassion, and justice (Kincheloe, 2004), and a full-lived curriculum (Aoki, 1989/1990).

FIVE

THE SEARCH FOR THE POETIC TEACHER

> Without thoughtful method, outcomes would be left solely to chance.
>
> David Hansen (2004, p. 120)

> "They are not college material," my mentor said during in-service week.
>
> "But, they must learn something," I replied.
>
> "Yeah, but don't sweat it. It can be a losing battle. This is just a holding tank more than anything else," he said.
>
> "But?" I looked baffled.
>
> He looked at me and said, "Be realistic. They will be lucky if they graduate, stay out of jail, and hold on to a job for more than six months at a time."

As Bill, my former mentor, finished those sentences, I remembered the day that I was told to be realistic about ever becoming an architect. One more time, I was told to be realistic about something, and this time it was about teaching and reaching out to students. This was actually very hard for me to reconcile.

As teachers, we enter the profession with goals, dreams, expectations, and desires for immense satisfactions and rewards (Hansen, 1998), seeking those spiritual experiences and moments that fulfill our lives and transform education into something meaningful (R. Miller, 1997). Dewey reminds us that such intellectual constructiveness cannot occur when children are imposed upon with problems and situations that do not belong to them and their lives. The everyday classroom, as he points out, is filled with problems that come from the teacher, making education artificial (see Dewey, 1916/1944, pp. 152–163). Hansen (2004) reminds us that education is based on engineering, methodology, and rules to achieve this end, as he clearly states:

> A poetics of teaching can help counter narrow, still prevailing views that cast teaching as merely an engineering problem of how to transfer a preset body of knowledge and skills efficiently to students. . . . When that happens, the well-documented consequences include teacher and student alienation, distorted understandings of what education means, and public confusion about what should occur in places set aside for learning. (Hansen, 2004, p. 121)

In many ways, Hansen is warning us of the danger of an education that merely seeks to deposit into students knowledge to be remembered for a test or an assignment. Such action does not translate into anything meaningful for the student, apart from the need to know it for a distant notion of the grade. Perhaps that is why I walked out on my students that day. I was tired of not getting the results that I wanted, as assignments went undone and homework was not turned in. I realized that I was not providing my students the education they needed, and it was hurting all of us.

I heard about David Hansen from Dr. Blake Bickham when we attended a class together, but I never paid much attention to him. That is until I had the chance to attend a conference where Hansen gave the keynote speech. After that, I decided to investigate and read some of his writing. While doing research, I came across Hansen's article *A Poetics of Teaching* (2004). Immediately, my breath was taken away. Hansen was telling me, the radical and revolutionary teacher, who was no longer radical or revolutionary, about the humanity of education and teaching. Yes, I read Freire's (1970) call for an end to banking education and the inhuman aspect of such practice on countless occasions. David Hansen, however, was telling me something more. I needed to be reminded that the students sitting in the classroom were humans and not empty vessels. For Hansen (2004), the students are individuals with their own vision of the world, dreams, and goals. The good teacher, in conclusion, is he or she that practices a form of teaching that goes "hand-in-hand with treating students as persons rather than as empty vessels in need of filling" (Hansen, 2004, p. 120).

What do the poetics of teaching mean to the critical pedagogue and the special education teacher? A friend of mine once told me that whenever he sits in an ARD (Admission, Review, and Dismissal) meeting, he gets the feeling that we are more interested in satisfying the need and the desires of parents than the needs of students. Perhaps this hits the center nerve of what education should be, which should be concerned with the need of the students only.

Hansen's poetics of teaching are not some romantic notion of what education should be. It is an urgent call, reminding us that we are indeed teaching human beings and autonomous individuals. Hansen (2004) defines poetics as a heightened awareness of the senses in the context of our surroundings. It is, as he points out (see Hansen, 2004, p. 122), an intensified feeling that we encounter in our natural and human world and an active response to what happens within us and around us. The poetic teacher, therefore, is he or she who actively responds to his or her natural and human world, becoming fully engaged with what occurs within the four walls of a classroom.

What does this active engagement mean? Poetics are metaphorical engagements (Hansen, 2004). Beyond mere linguistics, Hansen makes it clear that this metaphor is a hermeneutical process of inquiry and understanding. This metaphor is not the distant grasping of one thing through the "agency" of something else; rather, it is the immediate hold of the "fundamentals" of something (Hansen, 2004, p. 128), transpiring into a moral education. Poetic teaching becomes a moral endeavor, and this means the departure from the teaching of distant knowledge that is irrelevant to students' lives. It is the understanding of "something about the student as a human being" (Hansen, 2004, p. 130). In the end, this is the appreciation of the students' presence, welcoming the students' contributions.

As a critical pedagogue who is trying to help the students make sense of the world they live, I realize that I must also become a poetic pedagogue. I must realize that I am teaching human beings, and I must welcome their presence, appreciating their contributions and celebrating what they bring. This is Hansen's message to us—critical pedagogues and special education teachers. The full-lived curriculum, for Hansen, is the curriculum of poetry in our metaphorical quest of what life really means.

SIX

CARING FOR THE WHOLE CHILD

What we teach is ultimately a reflection of why we teach.

Elliot Eisner (2006, p. 44)

I agree with Purpel (1989) that education and school have become the worst form of social engineering. Somewhere along the line, we stopped questioning the current landscape of schools, requiring teachers to teach six to seven hours a day, students to endure eight hours of constant instruction, and classrooms composed of twenty- to thirty-something students. Society accepted the fact that the four core subjects, English, Math, natural and social sciences, would become the gauge for determining a student's academic potential. We, the public, determined that a test score would be the basis of properly measuring a child's ability to succeed in life. Society, without any significant challenge, has accepted that the proxies for validating a child's success was a series of measurements foreign to real life outside of school (Eisner, 2001). Society decided to avoid any significant intellectual debate regarding the current state of schools. At some point, we stopped asking and wondering about this construction of the school setting (Purpel, 1989). As Eisner points out, we became very clear in what we want schools to achieve in terms of numbers and literacy, but not much else (Eisner, 2002).

As a teacher, I have to admit that schools have become the worst place for collegiality and camaraderie. During my first year of teaching, it profoundly struck me to see how little opportunity for intellectual growth schools have to offer. It is here where, as a critical pedagogue, I am taking Eisner to heart when he says:

> The deeper problems of schooling have to do with teacher isolation and the fact that teachers don't often have access to other people who know what they are doing when they teach and who can help them do it better. (Eisner, 2001, p. 369)

It is a foolish idea and a naïve notion to attempt to foster a learning environment for students when that same luxury is denied to teachers. Society has been demanding excellence from teachers for a very long time. Nevertheless, it denies educators the opportunities and the resources to develop such excellence (Purpel, 1989). One may have to wonder and ask the question: How exactly are teachers going to excel in their job when they are offered so little resources? (Eisner, 2001).

Eisner puts it best when he says "activities in which youngsters participate in classes are the means through which the thinking is produced" (Eisner, 2001, p. 370). It is undeniable that what happens inside the classroom will shape a child's view of the world. Whether we want to accept it or not, the activities in which we engage the students in the classroom do matter, and this will be something they will take with them for the rest of their lives. So, how do we improve schools?

Purpel (1989) argues that school reforms have been trivial, concentrating on pay issues, instruction efficiency, and administrative procedures. Any serious concern for the social and cultural nature of education has been left aside. When it comes to students, Eisner (2001) reminds us that we are more preoccupied with a preparation to pass tests, which can only tell us how well they will do in future tests (see Eisner, 2001, p. 369). If the function of schools is to have any relevance in the student's life, what they learn, therefore, must transcend from the inner walls of the classroom into the openness of the outer world. Liss (2003) stated that he prefers a classroom in which students are not so concerned with the answer, but with the innumerable possibilities of the question. This is the exact call that Eisner makes when says, "intellectual achievement is not so much in problem solving, but in question posing" (Eisner, 2001, p. 370).

Education needs to do a lot more than to prepare students to pass tests. Schools will only reach the whole child when we teach them how to transfer the knowledge they learn in the classroom to the outside world. We are clearly doing the student a disservice when learning becomes "a hurdle to jump over" (Eisner, 2001, p. 370). If we are to improve schools, we need a vision of school that allocates the space and time for the student to pursue his or her interest, and we must create classrooms that spark the students' satisfaction. If we keep on concentrating on testing, as Eisner states, "we may win the battle and lose the war" (Eisner, 2001, p. 370).

Eisner is calling for the teaching of the whole-child. What does that mean? With the creation of the first graded school in Boston in 1859, society decided that children would sit in rows, master a series of courses, pass a class, and move on to the next grade level (Eisner, 2005; Zinn, 2003). Society also decided that the rigid disciplinary expectations of the workplace would transfer to the school (Zinn, 2003). Nevertheless, schools have done very little in promoting spaces where students create, wonder, and desire. The result has meant the creation of classrooms where students solve distant and irrelevant problems (Eisner, 2005; Dewey 1916/1944). Despite the fact that I was certified as a social studies teacher, my first teaching job was to teach fundamental math to special education students. I still remember their excitement every Friday when we played Monopoly™ or Money™. They worked hard every week to finish everything, so we could play on Fridays. They engaged in it with fervor as they learned to use money through a game. By playing a simple game, math became real to them.

Eisner's call to teach the whole-child means the creation of places where the humanity side of education would take place. This would mean going beyond the measurement index (Eisner, 2005), by recognizing what the students bring with them to the classroom. It would also mean transcending the barriers currently imposed in the system and create places for human growth. Teaching the whole-child means seeking a holistic education, which means creating true human spaces within our four walls. Fridays were not days when we only played money games. It was a time when we shared our lives and what was important for us. It was not uncommon for those who did not play, including myself, to gather and talk about anything and everything. Teaching the whole-child could mean a variety of things such as truly educating the child in his or her wholeness.

Nevertheless, as a critical pedagogue, I wonder what that really means at the end of the day. What does it entail to have a more human education, tapping creativity, or getting to know the student? In my quest for social justice, perhaps it signifies recognizing that schools need to become humanized institutions. In our need to better understand the school and its human potential, perhaps it is time to recognize that schools were invented with very inhuman goals in mind, such as mastering a passing grade and excelling in a state-mandated test (Apple, 1995; R. Miller, 1990/1997; Purpel, 1989). Eisner (2001) poses the question of what would happen if standardized tests ceased to exist. Perhaps we would be creating curriculums where the intellectual significance of the child would be what really matters. For a critical pedagogue like myself, in the end, teaching the whole child means creating opportunities for student satisfaction. This would mean an endless number of possibilities. This would mean to transcend academic measurability for those precious moments where we can reach each other beyond the academic boundaries.

SEVEN

THE SEARCH FOR THE FULL-LIVED CURRICULUM

> For mother, her hand will ever be there, and even in those times when hand does not touch, there is a touching that flows from the mother's care to the child.
>
> Ted Aoki (1989/1990, p. 8)

Leaving Argentina when I was only seven was perhaps one of the most pivotal and transcendental experiences in my life. It is hard to recollect all of the feelings that I had at that time, but I knew that I was leaving something behind for good. There are many cherished moments that I recall and treasure about Argentina. However, the relationship that I had with my first grade teacher is the one thing that I treasured the most. When I talked over the phone to my first grade teacher, Ernestina de Torrecilla, at the age of twenty, the first thing she said was, "I still remember when I grabbed your hand for the first time and taught you how to write."

Like everyone else, I can barely remember any of my teachers from my primary and secondary years, unless I use great amounts of efforts. However, it is my first-grade teacher who comes to my mind, effortlessly, when I think of somebody who has influenced me or touched my life. She was a person who took the time to welcome me into her classroom with a glowing smile on the same day that my Dad and her husband were leaving for a year to work in the oilfields of Brazil.

When we talk about a half-lived and a full-lived curriculum (Aoki, 1989/1990), what do we mean? The idea of a full-lived curriculum can yield many connotations. It lends itself to a plethora of interpretations and metaphors, and it can become a symbolic exercise vested in an endless maze of theoretical guessing. We can definitely take a critical pedagogy approach and decide that a full-lived curriculum means allowing the student to move beyond the facts (Kincheloe, 2002), by allowing him or her understand his or her cultural world (Kincheloe, 2004). We can say it is a radical approach to understanding the political, social, and economical connotations of the school life (McLaren, 2003c). We can also say it is a way to penetrate the student's lived world, and we can allow his or her interpretation of the world to be the basis of what happens in the classroom (Greene, 2003). We can also say that it means reclaiming the public in the public schools from the corporate takeover of the classroom (Giroux, 2003a). Or, it can mean looking at school through the poetics of humanism that school has to offer through the lives of those who make that school (Aoki, 1977, 1983, 1989/1990). Before defining a full-lived curriculum, perhaps, it is best to define and see what the half-lived curriculum looks like.

I can confidently say that my experience as an architecture student was a full-lived curriculum. I still remember, as an undergrad, how irritated we became when, during our first year as architecture students, we were not allowed to come up with models resembling buildings. Everything had to be abstract. Despite our eagerness to draw floor plans, exteriors, and interiors, we were discouraged from doing so. We would build models of cubes, lines, and symmetrical shapes in the abstract. Professors would also become irritated when our models remotely resembled anything like a building. We were told to go back to more abstract thinking. As the years passed, those exercises helped me understand the relation of spaces in ways I could have never conceived if I was told to simply start drawing floor plans. In many ways, we were learning to live those spaces. We were learning to design intellectually what made the being in a building (Aoki, 1989/1990).

As I progressed in the program, the rendering of the space would dictate the form of the building. This was an exercise that allowed us to understand the "multifold" of the building (Aoki, 1989/1990, p. 3). When one of my professors, an architect, was in a reform commission for schools in low-income neighborhoods, he told us how he repeatedly told the board how they can never build a good school until they understood the people in it. In my senior year of architecture, we took great pains in understanding the occupant of the spaces, where they came from, who they were, and what they wanted to do with it.

Aesthetics was a physical manifestation of understanding the universe of the space. A half-lived curriculum in architecture would have meant creating spaces without any notion of the space's purpose. Worst of all, it would have been creating spaces not understanding who was going to occupy it and why.

I agree with Aoki (1989/1990) that we constantly call for excellence and that such a call has become a popular stance. For us during architecture school, excellence meant understanding what that space was to be. I understand that as a critical pedagogue in search of the full-lived curriculum excellence can and will denote an array of things. Nevertheless, for Aoki, to excel means fully grasping what the school and the teacher are to be, by surpassing what one is and attempting to reach what one desires to become. As Aoki explains, "to excel can be understood as a coming to a deeper understanding of who we are and moving beyond" (Aoki, 1989/1990, p. 5). As we can see, for Aoki, excelling means having a deep understanding of what it would take to make us a better human being. The full-lived curriculum is an understanding that life and school are not two separate entities. It is the recognition that what occurs in the classroom affects the children's lives outside the school. The need to make school and life a single entity is more urgent now than ever.

What is the point of all this for the critical pedagogue? Aoki (1989/1990) calls the standard curriculum "curriculum-as-planned" (Aoki, 1989/1990, p. 10). Curriculum-as-planned is what, in essence, schools have become, where a standard curriculum dictates what students learn in order to pass a test. The full-lived curriculum is human curriculum allowing students and teachers a more profound hermeneutical quest. This can mean a variety of things. Nevertheless, let me illustrate a point. When I was an architecture undergrad, the construction of a final model in architecture school was a lengthy process of trial and error. We knew that we would be making countless mock-up models before the jury would see the final model. The full-lived curriculum is learning in which the students know that trials and errors are part of the process. The full-lived curriculum allows for failure, as it is an integral part of living. The half-lived curriculum is the standardized curriculum that heavily penalizes failure in the form of grades, promotions, and punishments for the evaluation of a student's progress (Purpel, 1989). The full-lived curriculum is the curriculum that allows the student to wonder, inquire, and explore the intimate dance between life and school. In this format, the struggles that we encounter are part of the spiritual process of learning (Aoki, 1989/1990). Again, this can mean different things to different people. For me, as a critical pedagogue, a full-lived curriculum is a clear denunciation of grades, rewards, punishment, promotions, and demotions. It is a denunciation of the pressures vested on students by standardized curriculum, and it is the firm criticism of the professional teaching environment where teachers are mere technocrats following prescribed instructions. The full-lived curriculum is, in the end, a serious intellectual quest which allows the teacher to be the spiritual guide and allows his or her students to exercise their own autonomy.

The full-lived curriculum is a human curriculum which allows the student and the teacher to forge intimate relationships for growth. A full-lived curriculum is not one that only allows for the dissemination of knowledge from an authority from above, but one that allows for the mutual construction of knowledge where teachers and students teach each other.

EIGHT

MY MICROSCOPIC VIEW

I was sitting in my counselor's office one day, and I finally said in anger, "I want to take drafting. I want to be an architect."

"I am going to do it no matter what," I finally blurted it out.

"Go ahead. Just remember when you start making F's that I told you so," my counselor said.

He went ahead and said, "You are going to have to be realistic about college once and for all. These endless conversations are starting to irritate me."

There were many frustrating moments during my first year of teaching. However, the most frustrating thing for me was to teach social studies. Having spent already three years in the graduate program, I knew that I wanted my class to be different, but I did not know how. I knew that something was not working, but I also learned that they were not conditioned to explore. All they wanted was conventional work and nothing else. However, the most striking thing to learn was that many of my students did not have many aspirations for the future. They never explored the possibility of attending college and having a career. In the same way that I experienced, they learned to believe that they should not expect too much out of life. And like myself, they had an aura of impossibility rendered on them, where disability is the synonym of incapability.

The need to explore a connection between disability and critical pedagogy surfaced during the spring of 2006 at the AERA conference in San Francisco. However, it took me two years to arrive at the crystallization of this topic. For quite some time, I have been reading about the pedagogy of liberation or conscientization (Freire, 1970/2000). It became clear to me that education was an oppressive relationship between teachers and students. In this environment, students are passive agents, reacting to the teachers' actions as the ultimate dispensers of knowledge. Freire defines this kind of education as "banking education," whose key motive is to create a "manageable being" (Freire, 1970/2000, p. 73). By manageable beings, Freire argues that education creates human beings unable to react and transform to the world around them. This means that the individual accepts a passive role, which impedes him or her from having a complete picture of reality. The consequence is that the individual cannot act as an independent and autonomous thinking being.

As a doctoral student in social education, I read Freire's (1970/2000) Pedagogy of the Oppressed many times. On my blue days, I read it with frustration and anger. On my bright days, I read it with ease, and everything made perfect sense. I knew that oppression was a key ingredient of special education; however, I was unable to make the connection with critical pedagogy in an articulate manner. I kept wondering: how are my students in special education oppressed? How am I, as a teacher and disabled, oppressed as well? What is it that makes special education into banking education? As a teacher, am I an oppressor? It was not easy for me to make sense of these questions. In addition, to some extent, it continues to be a hard task for me to this day.

One of the key tenets of critical pedagogy is to affirm that the oppressor treats the oppressed as marginal (Freire, 1970/2000, p. 74). When I decided to pursue a connection between critical pedagogy and disability, I was not sure how to do it. In my heart, I knew that if there was somebody regarded as marginal, it was the disabled (Oliver, 1992). The oppressor treats the oppressed as an outsider to society (Freire, 1970/2000), which is something familiar to the disabled (Oliver, 1992; Stiker, 1999). Historically, disabled people were sacrificed and were exposed to decay (Covey, 1998; Osgood, 2005). Until recently, scores of disabled were shunned from society (Hehir, 2005).

Everything changed for me one day when I returned from San Francisco. I was working in the special education office when suddenly another teacher said, "I hate it when they talk. My perfect day is when they simply sit down, shut their mouth, and get to work." At that time, memories from the immediate past started to resurface. I started to remember when one teacher just told me that special education students were lazy and told me to be realistic about "them." I remembered when the diagnostician told me I was the "big" exception to the rule. Once, a teacher told me they (disabled students) were lucky if they keep a job for six months. This teacher said that their big chance in life was the military. I also remembered the countless times when my high school counselor told me to be realistic about ever going to college or architecture school. I remember that at one point I was not considered "college material." I realized that even within the walls of special education, "disabled" was a synonym of "marginalized" (Freire, 1970/2000), and over the years, I became to see special education as a benevolent and paternalistic welfare state with the never-ending feeling of people thinking that it is the disabled students' fault that they are disabled.

Pedagogy of the disabled emerged out of the need to make the connection between disability and Freire's theory of conscientization or liberation (Darder, et al., 2003). It means understanding the hidden forces of the current reality and validating possible alternatives to the current state of things (Kincheloe, 2004). Nevertheless, I struggled with concepts of dehumanizing education and oppression in special education. I am a firm believer in the inclusion of special children in the regular class (Hehir, 2005; Reiser, 2006b). However, hair pulling and gut wrenching questions started to emerge. How do we give a voice to the deaf and mute? Do we include in the classroom he or she who wets diapers or drools constantly? Where do we draw a line? How do I reconcile my own feelings about being disabled with the fact that I never wanted to be associated with disabled students when I was in high school? Despite having such questions, I did not know how to articulate my argument. I firmly adhered to the notion that special education kept the disadvantaged marginalized in the current state of affairs, and I struggled to visualize just how.

Vignettes of a Human Pedagogy

I was born with cerebral palsy. When my mom was pregnant and on vacation, she had an accident while crossing a snowy street in Chile. I turned upside down inside the womb. A military medic, who was also on vacation, helped my mom survive the critical first 48 hours as she had convulsions, high fever, and almost lost me. Once my parents were back in Argentina, doctors suggested an abortion. My mom insisted on giving birth to me. During a routine check, an inexperienced resident broke the amniotic sack and caused my mom to go prematurely into labor. In the commotion, I lost oxygen to the brain during the drug-induced and forced labor. Once I was born, nurses were unable to detect whether I was breathing or not, so they literally started to punch me. After they stopped beating me, I was officially declared dead by doctors. The hospital's nun and chaplain on duty discovered that I was actually alive, as they were giving me my last rites. My dad placed his glasses on my nose, and they discovered that I was actually breathing. I was so small that they kept me in an incubator for three months. I was paralyzed from the neck downward, until I was two, and until I was four, my legs were paralyzed.

I still remember the day my student Adam [not his real name] complained about math class and the assignments. He asked me, "Why are you teaching this stuff that is so difficult?" Adam said afterwards, "This is second grade . . . you know." I asked him whether he was a second grader, and he said he was not. He told me he was a ninth grader. I said, "So . . . we don't do second grade stuff here." In many ways, Adam refused to acknowledge his disability. Life, for a disabled person, can best be described as a kaleidoscope of emotions. We acknowledge we have limitations, but we deny that we are disabled (Gabel, 2002). We construct our own notions of the world, by constructing an aesthetic of ourselves, as Dewey (1934) argues. The lives that we live, including our surroundings and experiences, shape our awareness of how we see ourselves. The contributions of our environment create our view and cultural frame of reference (Kincheloe, 2004). McLaren (2003b) argues that culture represents the formation, inculcation, and perpetuation of "particular forms of social life" (pp. 186–187). This is what Gabel (2002) defines as the creation of a "sense of self," which allows us to construct our images of who we are (p. 181).

Gabel (2002) talks about the experience she had with her daughter, a mentally retarded person. Although her daughter acknowledged her limitations, she refused to conceive the notion she was disabled (see Gabel, 2002, pp. 180–181). Her daughter did not use her limitations to construct her identity. As a result, Gabel's daughter used a dialectical or aesthetic process that enabled her to construct a meaning of the self independently from outside influences. As I said, my childhood was normal. I climbed trees, played sports, wrote, and did everything that a child would do. This meant that, for a long period of my life, my disability was not an issue. I overcame obstacles naturally. For example, my handwriting was not clear, so I simply practiced by copying pages out of books by hand. I would read aloud to my older sister to practice my speech. Until I was a teenager, my limitations were not obstacles that impeded me from doing what I wanted, but minor setbacks that I needed to correct through hard work. I was part of a living pedagogy (Dewey, 1944; Gabel, 2002).

Gabel discusses that she allowed her daughter to develop her own identity as an African-American, despite the fact that her heritage also includes Japanese (see Gabel, 2002, p. 181). This allowed her daughter the freedom to understand her own life in her own terms as an African-American. During my high school years, I constantly argued with my counselor about taking drafting, so I could prepare myself for engineering or architecture school. I never desisted from studying architecture. My parents were supportive of the idea, and they encouraged me to pursue my goal. At times, they were the only ones saying yes when everyone else said no. At home, I was part of a living pedagogy that enabled me the freedom to understand my life, allowing me to decide for myself the course of my own life. If I had given in to my counselor's efforts to make me desist from studying what I wanted, how would that have damaged my pedagogical experience of seeing myself as capable?

Despite the argument that disabled people are able to construct their own identity, it is well acknowledged that disability renders the social stigma of incapacity (Hehir, 2005; Longmore, 1995). Society has created a culture of disablement in dealing with disability (Baylies, 2002). At times, this is an unforgiving culture that reminds us that we are disabled (Clare, 2001). Ho (2004) describes that the experience of labeling somebody disabled is an act that carries marginalization connotations. When conflicts arose with my teachers in seventh grade in Venezuela, my dad decided to request a transfer to another country. Some teachers refused to work with me, and other teachers threatened to fail me on purpose. A colleague of my father suggested that he request a transfer to the United States. He pointed to the fact that in the United States there were laws and regulations protecting disabled students. In the fall of 1983, we were transferred to the United States.

In the United States, everything changed. We can say things became better, as I was given modifications and accommodations for the first time. However, things also changed for the worse. My disability, once a simple abnormality to overcome, became the epicenter of who I was and how I was defined (Ho, 2004). In the United States, my disability became my identity, which dictated the course of action taken by teachers and counselors. Once, I was simply somebody else in the crowd, who just needed some help in achieving some tasks. After we arrived in the U.S., I was officially a disabled. For the first time in my life, I was attending different classes, in separate places, and away from the rest. The rationale, from the school officials, was that my grades were not as good as we originally thought, and I needed to take some remedial courses. As a result, I was placed in resource level courses.

Ho (2004) asserts that such marginalization provokes great resistance from parents and students, who realize the oppressive nature of special education. It was the first time that my disability was a deficit (Gabel, 2002). Once in the U.S., I experienced an entire shift on my definition of myself. Before, I was simply impaired; I merely had an attribute that limited me physically. In the U.S., I was disabled, which meant I was socially labeled and categorized as someone who was not on equal footing with everyone else (Burchardt, 2004). This experience, for me, was devastating, and over the years, this became an example of what a living pedagogy is not.

NINE

PEDAGOGY OF AFFECTION

I will never forget the way Ms. Torrecilla connected with the students so affectionately. I remember how she made sure we had our coats buttoned before we left for home in the wintertime, how she made sure we ate our lunches, and how she helped everyone get ready for physical education class. She used to say that she was our second mother, and school was our second home. It was not uncommon for us, as students, to greet or say goodbye to Ms. Torrecilla with a hug. She was one of the best examples of the pedagogy of humanity.

Blaine Hatt (2005) calls this the pedagogy of love. In that sense, pedagogy of love is the ability of the teacher to transcend the mere professional requisites of the profession and establish a close relationship with his or her students. This is the call for every teacher to assume a parental responsibility in pedagogy (Hatt, 2005). For many of us, Ms. Torrecilla was our mother, as she exemplified the teacher who recognizes that cognitive needs are not mere instructional requirements, but a loco parentis relation between teacher and student. Hatt (2005) defines this relationship between teacher and student as "pathic," meaning that this is the pedagogy of love, affection, and feeling (p. 672). Pedagogy of humanity is love, which unites the teacher with his or her pupils.

Ms. Torrecilla never saw me as disabled, but as a capable being. She taught me how to read and write. She encouraged me to play and participate in the school's olympiad. During college, she was the one who called or wrote to encourage me when I was distressed. She never doubted that I was going to graduate from architecture school, contrary to the opinion of many people in my high school. For her, I was not deficient. For Gabel (2002), to label someone disabled is to reaffirm the notion that "something innately" is deficient (p. 182). In the end, disability is a label that renders social oppression. In other words, it is society which has placed an institutional "disabling" attitude on the disabled (Oliver, 1992, p. 112). Disability, then, becomes a social marker signifying one's place in the world. As a result, such a marker can greatly influence the way the disabled sees himself or herself, dictating the degree of capability one is willing to accept.

Pedagogy of Oppression

My fascination with technical drawing, or drafting, started early in my life. I grew up in a family of engineers. Since I was a little kid, I saw my grandfather, dad, and uncle design and perform all sorts of experiments. It was not uncommon for me to watch my father draw technical plans of the projects he was working at any given time. As a little kid, he used to give me a ruler and a pencil, so I could draw as well, while providing him some company. By the time I was a teenager, I knew I wanted to study a career involving drafting, whether it be architecture or mechanical engineering. However, not everyone shared my passion and my dream, and during my high school years, I would be discouraged from pursuing such a dream.

In response to disability as a form of social repression, Oliver (1986) developed the social model of disability. Developed in the U. K. (Mitra, 2006), the social model contends that disability is a social construction which renders the disabled individual incapable, believing that individuals are unable to "participate fully in society" (Oliver, 1986, p. 6). Within that framework, the treatment of the disabled is viewed as an oppressive act (Abberley, 1987). The social model contends that disability is a social construction, and society places limits on the disabled through the social, political, economical, and cultural construction of barriers (Baglieri & Knopf, 2004; Reiser, 2006b). Therefore, society views the disabled as a limited and incapable person. The social model shifted society's perception of disability from the medical model, which conceives disability as a problem within the individual as a human characteristic (Baglieri & Knopf, 2004), to the concept that disability is an oppressive barrier vested on the disabled.

According to Gabel (2002), when we label someone disabled, we acknowledge that someone is "oppressed" (p. 182). It renders the notion that someone has been discriminated against and that "barriers" are presented which discourage the disabled from "equal participation" (Reiser, 2006b, p. 137). In Venezuela, I started to experience problems with my knees. I could not run fast enough. When we played baseball, I was the umpire, and I was the goalie, when we played soccer. When we played volleyball, I permanently served the ball. Somehow, I was accommodated to participate. In the U.S., I was excluded from regular PE. For someone who was used to being the regular goalie or the umpire, taking adaptive PE, where we only played board games or shuffleboard, was a denigrating experience. The thought that I could not join the rest of my peers was devastating. In this framework, Reiser (2006b) regards disability as the "loss or limitations of opportunity" to fully participate in society (p. 135). His view is that society has created a view of the disabled as different, by conceiving us as less human and not accepting our participation. Through fear and prejudice, the disablement of the human becomes a social act of ideology.

To view disability as a social ideology of oppression has significant and important consequences. It is to accept that society has dehumanized us (Freire, 1970/2000). This is the perception that society has a better understanding of the disabled and can offer a better solution. In my own experience, the solution was for others to convince me to desist from my desires of becoming an architect. In the end, the social model is about empowerment. It is the realization that barriers are socially constructed. In the end, the social model has been the disabled community's response to oppression.

The social model of disability was based on Marxist theory, and denunciation of capitalism (Abberley, 1987). The roots are based on the struggle of the disabled to fight for their rights in a capitalistic society (Burchardt, 2004). It has been embraced mostly in the UK by certain academics and disability advocates (Mitra, 2006). Despite promoting an ideology of struggle for the emancipation of the disabled, disability advocates and academicians in the field do not seem to reach a consensus of what would be a liberating pedagogy. Questions regarding what would embody inclusion and who should be included continue to linger. Doubt exists in terms of how the disabled can have a voice (Gabel, 2002). Although the social model and critical pedagogy could form the perfect alliance for liberating the disabled from oppression, skepticism remains the norm.

TEN

OBSTACLES TO CONSCIOUSNESS

My brother and I grew very close. Because of his abilities, my brother jumped two years ahead scholastically. My parents thought it was best for me to be in the same grade level, so I was held back a year. Until we went to college, we were always in the same grade. Before coming to the U. S., we took the same classes and had the same teachers. Once we were here, we were separated. He was placed in the regular and honor curriculum, and I was placed in the special education track. The experience was traumatic to me for a long time. My brother was no longer part of my life in school. I was by myself for the first time. He was in one place, and I was in another. We had different classes, different lunches, and different teachers. Once, he was part of my daily life in school. In the U. S., I did not see him until we were ready to go home in the afternoon.

The numbers do not lie. There are 500 million people in the world considered disabled, according to the United Nations (see Reiser, 2006b, p. 140). According to Erevelles (2002), there are "49 million" Americans labeled as disabled in this nation (p. 7). These are individuals that historically have faced discrimination (Erevelles, 2002; Ferri & Connor, 2005; Oliver & Zarb, 1989; Russell, 1998; Stiker, 1999). Despite the overwhelming consensus that people with disability have been socially oppressed throughout history, the discourse of disability has been polarized.

Over the last two decades, the discourse of disability has been polarized between the medical model and the social model (Baglieri & Knopf, 2004; Barnes, 2003; Reiser, 2006b; Tregaskis, 2004). The medical model contemplates the disabled as a problem that needs to be fixed and corrected. On the other hand, the social model looks at the social ideologies that place limitations on the disabled. Nevertheless, serious questions regarding the moral entity of disability have been raised (Danermark & Gellerstedt, 2004; Erevelles, 2002; Howe & Miramontes, 1991; Paul, French, & Cramston-Gingras, 2001). This has hampered the discourse of disability to reach a consensus of what constitutes a liberating pedagogy for the disabled.

The social model of disability was designed to address questions like the one I faced when I was separated from my brother. Why was I not normal anymore? Why was I placed in special classes? Is it enough for me to feel normal and perceive myself as non-disabled when society thinks I am not? After all, I do have limitations. For example, I need help getting my food in a buffet line, and I do need help getting a drink, when the glasses or cups are too small.

The struggle of every social model proponent has been to erase the social barriers of the disabled, and the struggle of every critical pedagogue has been to eradicate the injustices of society. However, we, as a society, still need to agree upon a viable alternative towards a liberating pedagogy for the disabled. In this section, I want to address two areas of concern for me, which lead to such disagreement: social oppression and citizenship.

Social Oppression

Abberley (1987) criticizes the social model for not being specific about the concept of oppression. According to him, the concept of oppression has been used as an "obvious" outcome in the treatment of the disabled; however, it has been "difficult to substantiate" (Abberley, 1987, p. 6). He proposed the need to define what oppression means for the disabled, and he argues that oppression for the disabled is not the same as oppression based on gender or sex. For Abberley (1987), assimilating all groups into the same category of oppression is not feasible, as he states that somebody "benefits" from racial and sexual oppression (Abberley, 1987, p. 16).

For Abberley, there are substantial differences when it comes to defining oppression of the disabled and other kinds of oppression. Sexual and racial oppression are categorized under "biological" differences (Abberley, 1987, p. 8). Social disadvantages are explained in terms of biological superiority and inferiority. For the disabled, on the other hand, the argument of the social model of oppression is constructed by the social concept of impairment. Abberley points out that the question of inferiority for the disabled arises from the social notion of the "issue of impairment" (Abberley, 1987, p. 8). His argument is that a biological definition of impairment leaves us with the notion that something is wrong with disability, which is something in need of correction.

Abberley proposes a different definition for the oppression of the disabled. He argues that impairment is part of an authentic "life form" (Abberley, 1987, p. 9). Disability cannot be erased or corrected, which is what the medical model proposes (Baglieri & Knopf, 2004). What Abberley proposes is that oppression for the disabled must be constructed within a social theory. His suggestion is, therefore, to understand the economical, political, and cultural aspects of oppression for the disabled. This is crucial for the "political development" of the disabled (Abberley, 1987, p. 8). In this context, the impairment is not something that needs to be corrected, and people would learn to live with their disability. For example, deaf people would not use hearing devices to correct their hearing loss, but would learn other methods, such as sign language that would allow them to accept their conditions of deafness. This picture can render the possibility of someone being disabled; however, he or she would be competent within his or her framework of life. Abberley argues that we, as a society, often have a vision of the disabled as someone who lives in poor housing, works in a low-paying job, and is disadvantaged socially and economically (see Abberley, 1987, p. 13). This can be a point of utter disagreement for the disabled people, like myself, who are professionally successful and competent.

Abberley's proposition is significant. However, questions regarding the true concept of oppression continue to puzzle me. As a disabled individual, it is obvious that I am very successful. After all, I am a professional who earned a doctoral degree, and I learned to live with my disability. In the end, Abberley's argument is an attractive rationale to understand the social barriers of the disabled. However, it raises many questions, and as such, creates an obstacle for reaching a consciousness for the disabled. How can we continue to explain the persistent oppression of women and minorities when the concept of biology is no longer viable? Is not the belief that a non-impaired person is superior to an impaired person also a biological construction? The area of oppression is not the only arena where disability is debated. Recently, the idea of what constitutes citizenship, justice, morality, and liberation for the disabled has been hotly contested.

Disability and Citizenship

A clear and concise pedagogy of consciousness for the disabled must entail the need to have full citizenship, which means creating a society that develops social goals for its members and the common good, while attaining their own individuality (Erevelles, 2002). Nevertheless, even within the disability studies community, people appear to be at odds about what constitutes citizenship for the disabled.

What constitutes citizenship for the disabled? This is, at least, a very important question for me. I was hired to teach social studies. My first teaching assignment was to teach resource history and government. This meant that the students taking that class were "off-track," that they were not going to take the state-mandated test. Following the state curriculum was not a big issue. Instead, I was told that what really mattered was for them to become good citizens. As far as the administration was concerned, I was to teach these students the fundamental mechanisms of the government, the need to vote, and the possibility of joining the military. One administrator told me, "These are students who are not going to college. They need another viable alternative after graduation."

In theory and practice, the offer sounded exciting. However, very soon I started to have questions. What was the school's view of citizenship? Why was citizenship for these students reduced to voting, the government, and the military? Was the vision of participating citizenship (e.g., the ability of social, political, and economical consciousness and even dissent) not part of these students' lives?

The neo-liberal practices of the last three decades have resurrected and fueled the debate of citizenship for the disabled. The discourse of citizenship focuses mainly on three areas. First, it involves the relationship between the "state and the individual" (Gilbert, Cochrane, & Greenwell, 2005, p. 287). Second, it evolves around the theme of "inclusion" and "exclusion." Finally, the discourse centers around "social status" and the benefits of such entitlement (see Gilbert, et al., 2005, p. 287). However, Gilbert and associates find the concept of citizenship problematic for disability studies. They argue that the idea of citizenship can have different connotations depending on the circumstances. For example, citizenship evolves around the binary of inclusion and exclusion, the concept of inequality, and the result of marginal status (see Gilbert, et al., 2005, p. 287). Furthermore, citizenship also encompasses welfare, material availability, and active participation. Adding to this confusion, one may began to wonder what all this entails for disability studies. What is active citizenship for the disabled?

Abberley (1987) is not the only one suggesting that concepts of oppression and marginalization are different for the disabled. An interesting argument to examine is that of Erevelles (2002), who criticizes liberal theorists of social justice for not formulating a concise concept of citizenship for the disabled. She accuses the radical theorists of not including any "sustained discussion of cognitive/severe disability in their contemporary theoretical work on citizenship" (Erevelles, 2002, p. 8). She further argues that these theorists (e.g., Rawls, 1971) have actually deployed concepts of disability that regard it as acceptable to perceive people with cognitive/severe disabilities as non-citizens. For Erevelles, the tenet of the social theory of citizenship stems from the notion that the individual must be a competent and rational self. For example, she describes Rawls's position, who defines a citizen as "a fully cooperating member of society. . . . [with] the capacity to understand, to apply, and to act from the public conception of justice" (quoted in Erevelles, 2002, p. 8). Therefore, it is permissible, for liberal social theorists, to consider the severely mentally disabled outside the concept of participating citizenship. For Erevelles (2005), this is the weakness of the liberal concept of citizenship.

Erevelles (2002) offers a new paradigm in the concept of citizenship for the disabled. In her context and definition, "binaries like male/female, non-disabled/disabled, straight/queer are not boundary conditions but fluid concepts that tend to blur the defining limits of citizenship" (Erevelles, 2002, p. 8). Her desire is to move away from social contract theories, which use ethical principles to achieve the "common good"; rather, she borrows Mouffe's (1996) concept of producing political identities. This concept avoids defining binaries of oppression amongst marginalized and privileged groups. Instead, Mouffe suggests "modifying their identity so as to bring about a new political identity" (quoted in Erevelles, 2002, p. 15; Mouuffe, 1996, p. 24). For Erevelles, the need is to move beyond the humanistic limitations of citizenship, which for her continues to linger within the binary of the normal/abnormal. She offers a "transgressive" form of citizens. She borrows from Butler (1993) and Haraway (1990) the removal of social constraints of citizenship, which continue to accept the norms of the "normal body." Instead, her proposal is to move beyond the skin and the physical limitations of autonomy and self. This would mean accepting the notion that through viable alternatives, such as technology, caregivers, and mechanical devices of communications, the disabled would gain the right to full citizenship and social participation (Erevelles, 2002). Within this argument, even people with severe cognitive disabilities would have a voice.

I will not argue with Erevelles's criticism of radical theories of social citizenry, nor I will embrace her notion of a new political identity. Neither will I endorse or criticize her position. Despite agreeing with her view that Rawls's (1971) theory of justice is problematic because it excludes those unable to display functional autonomy to act upon society, I contend that Erevelles is symptomatic of the field of disability studies and the social model. It has become a field unable to reach an agreement of what would encompass citizenship for the disabled. Social model proponents agree in the basic assumption that disabled people are victims of oppression, and they are keen to assert the notion that the disabled are part of a different category from those suffering oppression on the basis of race, gender, or culture. For those trying to reach a level of conscientization for the disabled, this can be problematic. Can a successful disabled person experience discrimination? Does a disabled black or Latino confront discrimination in one area and not in others? How do we define participatory citizenship for an autistic or severely retarded person? These are questions that, despite Erevelles's best intentions, continue to be unanswered.

Going back to my social studies class, I decided that on Fridays we would have round tables where we would discuss issues. The students were reluctant at first, but they became engaged as time went on. They started to express their feelings about things such as the presidential race, sweatshops, and the military. Although I disagreed at times with them, I realized that these were people with something to say, and they had different points of view to express. Even more importantly, these students showed me that they were capable of engaging in elaborate arguments and debates, which contradicted the view held by some teachers and administrators from the special education department (Hehir, 2005).

The area of citizenship is not the only area where the need to reach conscientization for the disabled runs into problems. A much-contested area of disagreement is whether or not critical pedagogy has a place in disability studies. When I started this project, my aim was to bridge the gap between the two. However, as I will discuss next, not everyone agrees with the notion that critical pedagogy and disability can, in fact, be related and make a coherent argument for the disabled.

ELEVEN

CONSCIENTIZATION OF THE DISABLED

Greene (2003) asserts the notion that education lacks a meaningful conversation for the common good, which is an essential part of critical citizenship. Even Erevelles (2002) agrees with this argument. Greene (2003) finds it problematic that "young people find it increasingly difficult to project a long-range future" (p. 109). As such, people have lost faith that education can keep the culture alive. People like Greene remind us that, in the end, education has lost its vision and purpose.

When I started to read critical pedagogy, this theory was more than a technique or a pedagogical tool. For some time, I conceived critical pedagogy as a way for education to regain its vision and purpose, and a way to create "free and creative human beings" (Greene, 2003, p. 344). This is what Gore (2003) refers to as pedagogy and empowerment. By empowerment, Gore (2003) suggests that the authoritative dichotomy between teacher and student be erased. Instead, the teacher, always perceived as an authoritative figure, would cede his or her power to the students. This would create an agency where power is "shared" for the purpose of learning (p. 344). The purpose of critical pedagogy is to empower students; however, not everyone shares this view. On the contrary, some authors (Erevelles, 2000; Gabel, 2002) have critically questioned the possible association of critical pedagogy and disability.

Gabel (2002) finds some conceptual problems in critical pedagogy. She wonders whether we can have a liberatory pedagogy for the disabled. She asks:

> Can we locate a pedagogy wherein the discourse is as liberatory as possible, while caring yet vulnerable and risky relations exist, and where pedagogical participants are narrators of their own texts? Will this pedagogy recognize and account for students and teachers of diverse ability? (Gabel, 2002, p. 184)

Furthermore, she wonders whether such pedagogy can include people with significant impairments or people who might need a substantial amount of assistance in their daily lives. These are provocative questions that would challenge any critical pedagogy proponent, including myself, opening a wide array of possibilities in this debate.

At the core of her argument, Gabel (2002) criticizes critical pedagogy for not addressing people with "different abilities," as she likes to call the disabled. In her critique of Freire's work, she argues that Freire's theory of liberation is insufficient for not considering disability theory (Gabel, 2002). She wonders how "critique and self-transformation play themselves out in the lives of self-identified disabled people" (Gabel, 2002, p. 185). She criticizes McLaren for not including the disabled in his list of oppressed people. In the end, she argues that critical pedagogues have tried to include a varied group of oppressed people while asserting a certain homogeneity in their ability. In the end, for Gabel, critical pedagogues have failed to propose a coherent pedagogy that includes the "differently" abled. This has left her with many questions regarding a liberatory pedagogy for people with different abilities. Who can be liberated? Who can have a voice? Does inclusion work for everyone?

I tend to agree with Gabel (2002) that even the most severely cognitively disabled person develops an autonomous identity. At this point, I do not intend to agree or disagree with Gabel about her critique of critical pedagogy. Rather, I see this as another attempt by social model proponents to classify the disabled as a unique case of oppression, which I find problematic.

Gabel is not the only one in disability studies who criticizes critical pedagogues. Erevelles (2000) also finds serious problems with critical pedagogy. In her articulation, she also criticizes people like McLaren or Giroux for not mentioning the disabled as an oppressed group. In that sense, Erevelles also argues that critical pedagogy is incomplete because it does not mention the disabled in any substantial way in its discourse of oppression (Erevelles, 2002). She finds critical pedagogy problematic when, within the radical possibilities of the theory, the disabled are excluded, or perceived to be so much outside the margins of oppression that liberation is impossible. In the end, we, as academics and educators, find ourselves, one more time, unable to reach a consensus of what would enable a liberatory praxis for the disabled.

Gabel (2002) argues that critical pedagogy cannot be inclusive, until people with different abilities are addressed. Her proposition is that every marginalized group has different needs, and that critical pedagogy must offer elasticity, and not an across-the-board uniformity, when addressing marginalized groups. Abberley (1987) proposes to start defining the political identities of the disabled when formulating concepts of oppression for the social model. Erevelles (2000) argues that for critical pedagogy to make sense, critical pedagogues must start accounting the repressive economical realities of the disabled in their argument against capitalism, and only when the materialistic/historical context of the disabled are included will critical pedagogy be a valid theory for Erevelles.

The obstacles for the conscientization of the disabled are many. Vital questions will always arise regarding what would constitute a liberatory praxis for the disabled. Is inclusion safe for everyone? Under what conditions can we make inclusion emotionally safe for the disabled? Even more importantly, does inclusion mean changing the disabled world-view? Or, does it mean changing the non-disabled view of disability? We may not have the answers to all these questions, and perhaps we will never reach such a point. However, I believe that the challenge of every special education teacher is to propose the vision of a society where disabled individuals are equal human beings, not marginal entities. A pedagogy for the disabled, with its possible tensions and contradictions, can offer that possibility. This is what Schön and Rein (1994) refer to as framing and reframing, which is the action of naming the parts or frames of constructed reality, along with the possibility of reflection or reframing to offer a better alternative. In the next section, using this concept of framing and reframing, I will discuss the possibility of a pedagogy for the disabled.

TWELVE

PEDAGOGY OF THE DISABLED

I was paralyzed from the neck downward, until I was four or so, and very few people know this. I could not use my arms or legs. Doctors told my mom that I was going to be a vegetable, and I was going to be lucky if I could ever speak, much less read and write. My Mom, however, never gave up. She decided to check out every book on physical therapy from the local library, and she became determined to make me walk. With the help of friends, she decided to fill an entire room with balloons. Every afternoon, she took me there, and she started to play with me. Little by little, I started to move my head, arms, and legs. And this is how I learned to walk at the age of four.

As I said before, I attempted not to agree or disagree with the critics of the social model and critical pedagogy in the previous section. I do find their points and arguments to be contentious and valid enough. However, I find their proposal problematic for those of us who are attempting to find a liberating pedagogy for the disabled. Questions regarding liberation, oppression, and conscientization for the disabled will always surface. People in favor of and against such a possibility will always flood our academic journals and bookshelves. We will always be puzzled by what can constitute a liberatory pedagogy for the severely cognitively disabled. Nevertheless, it is within the beauty of this struggle that I will put forward the argument for a liberatory pedagogy of the disabled.

Leaving the Crutches Behind

Partly due to fear, partly due to my walking disability, and honestly, partly due to drawing attention to myself like any other five year old would do, until the age of five or six, I occasionally used crutches and a cane. In my kindergarten in Argentina, there was this giant slide in the playground that everybody wanted to ride. Along with the old locomotive, it was the main attraction in the playground. You could go up the ladder to run the slide, but this was not how we did it. In order to get to the top and run down the slide, we climbed the adjacent tree. At the age of five or six, climbing that tree during recess to ride the giant slide was our daily act of bravado.

Like everything else in my early life, I just stood there and watched everyone else play, as I was not allowed to either climb the tree or ride the slide. That is until one day my kindergarten teacher told me to go ahead and climb. I was scared at first, but she insisted, and I did it. I never used a cane again, until I broke my knee while playing flag-football in college.

I find Erevelles' and Gabel's arguments problematic. What does Gabel (2002) mean by pedagogy of the self? What does Erevelles (2002) mean by the deconstruction of liberal theory of individuality as it pertains to the disabled? Furthermore, what does Erevelles (2000) attempt to insinuate by suggesting a critical pedagogy that would render visible the materialistic structures of oppression for the marginalized? Again, finding answers to these questions can be as contentious as the questions that we propose. However, we can always dwell in the beauty of wrestling with these questions.

When I decided to implement a round table discussion on Fridays, my goal was to empower my students. I persisted despite the obvious resistance that I encountered from my students. Nevertheless, after some time, we found ourselves wrestling with all kinds of questions and debates. We might never know how successful we were. However, I took the effort to know my students' voices. For one hour every week, they were able to express their anger, desires, doubts, and their view of the world. This is something that many students do not have the opportunity to do in today's public schools. My personal experience as a special education teacher reminds me that every child, even those with severe cognitive disabilities, has something to say and something to express.

One area that I find problematic is Gabel's (2002) argument about critical pedagogy's notion of liberating voice. For Gabel, the metaphoric use of voice in critical pedagogy is troublesome. It leaves unanswered questions about giving a voice for those who do not have a voice. Troubling as it is, the validity of Gabel's argument does not erase fundamental questions regarding what we want to achieve in the classroom. Fundamental to my attempt to establish a round table discussion was the need to address the important issues and struggles of our times (White & McCormack, 2006). Yes, in the area of disability we will always wrestle with the issue of who can have a voice, and under what conditions. Do we avoid the argument of figuring out how to give a voice to every disabled child? I hope not.

I am a firm believer that every child has something to say. Furthermore, I want to believe that scholars in disability are educated enough to realize that there are tools that every teacher can adapt to his or her needs and use it in his or her field. To further expand this argument, I want to believe that these scholars have enough vision to realize that academics, such as Freire, did not have to include the disabled in his list of marginalized people. Again, I want to believe that people in the academia of disability studies have sufficient vision to realize that Freire was talking about the oppressed in the broadest of terms for the benefit of everyone, including the disabled.

Critical pedagogy is the pedagogy of possibility. This is the possibility that empowers the student to contextualize his or her world (Greene, 2003). By this, Greene emphasizes the need for the student to rediscover himself or herself. This is what Freire (1970/2000) calls liberation or the ability of the student to engage in a dialectical process. In other words, it is the ability to establish a dialogue. Within this faith, I want to propose a pedagogy of the disabled based on the pedagogy of possibility.

When Marcia (not her real name) called me by my first name in school, an assistant principal, who happened to be in the proximity, told her that she should address me as mister. I had to explain to the administrator that she was a former co-worker from my part-time job. Therefore, it was difficult for her to address me as mister. During my first two years, colleagues and administrators criticized me for being too friendly with students. I utterly disagreed with them. Instead, I want to believe that I was interested in their lives and who they were. Was I deviating from my position of authority as a teacher? Absolutely not. However, I was firm in my conviction that the students were human beings, and that they needed to see me as a human being as well. That is why, to this day, I still share with my students my favorite music, the fact that I also have a portable MP3 player, and what I think of the latest movie I saw on the weekend.

During my first year, on purpose, during our conversations on Fridays, I let the conversation divert in any direction. We started talking about slavery in the South, and we ended talking about the places from which we would buy our clothes. Perhaps I did it intentionally, so we could explore current examples of slavery disguised in the concept of sweatshops and cheap retailing stores. However, at some level, I was also interested in their stories, and I was interested in sharing mine. Pedagogy of the disabled is the pedagogy of possibilities, which starts by sharing who we are.

Greene (2003) reminds us that critical pedagogy's fundamental function is to create freethinking humans. When I was hired, I was told not to expect too much out of the group of students that I was going to teach. They were not going to college. They were not particularly interested in school either. They just wanted to learn something they could use in their life. As the round table discussion went on, I realized that these students had something to share and say. They had ambitions for their future, and they possessed a world vision of their own, just like everyone else. I believe that they never had the time and the space to share those visions. The pedagogy of the disabled must start by creating those spaces where students can express themselves freely. Perhaps, even more importantly, it is the ability of everyone to get to know each other (Bell, Washington, Weinstein, & Love, 2003).

I am truly convinced that people are afraid of possibilities. Gabel (2002) talks about her daughter's autonomous decision to view herself as a non-disabled. Nevertheless, later Gabel describes how she and her husband decided that inclusive education was not in the best interest of her daughter. Gabel argues that in the decision to preserve certain family structures and a safe environment, she and her husband decided to place their daughter in a separate education track (see Gabel, 2002, p. 189). It is not my work to agree or disagree with Gabel's decision to place her daughter in special settings because of her severe mental retardation. However, I do question her fear. It is ironic that as someone who questions critical pedagogy for not emancipating the disabled enough in its praxis of liberation, we see Gabel actually justifying her position in preserving a restricted and safe environment for her own daughter.

During my teaching career, I have had the privilege of teaching several autistic and savant students. I will never know how much I truly reached them, or whether I even make a difference in their lives. These are students, however, independent enough to express themselves in their own way, which I find fascinating. If we are to advance a pedagogy for the disabled, we must conquer our fears. Perhaps instead of questioning whether a mute savant can have a voice, we should be asking ourselves what transformation we can devise that would provide the disabled with the opportunity to have a voice. Rather than articulating the limits of a particular disability, we should be putting forward elements that would erase the limiting barriers.

Juan was an emotionally disturbed student of mine, and it was very hard to speak and share his life. He was also terrified to go into the cafeteria and public spaces where there was a multitude. However, he drew beautifully, and I allowed him to do every assignment in the form of drawing. When he was allowed to draw, an entire world of creativity was unleashed in him. I wonder what would have happened if I insisted that he turn in his assignments in a conventional form. Deep in my heart, I want to believe that his drawings were his voice, and through his drawings, I got to know more of him. I want to believe that a liberating pedagogy of the disabled is about unleashing the shackles of oppression. A liberating pedagogy for the disabled that continues to roam in the impossibilities of certain limitations is not liberating.

As I said, I was terrified that day in kindergarten when I ruined my uniform with tempera paint. When my student, Mike (not his real name), broke a calculator I bought for math, he also was terrified. This calculator was one of many, which I bought in a dollar store for my math class. He pleaded with me not to write him up or call home; he said his mom would kill him. Ever since I was little, I had a fascination with dismantling things. My parents would give me old typewriters or radios for me to pull apart. So, Mike was stunned when I took a set of mini-tools from my desk, sat by him, and started to dismantle the calculator. I learned that Mike also liked to do the same thing. By the end of the school year, Mike and I pulled apart all the calculators I bought, dismantled three headphone sets, and dissembled an old computer that the wood shop teacher had in a corner.

Pedagogy for the disabled is about having fun. The special education student is crying, yelling, and screaming to have fun. Perhaps, that was why everyone looked forward to playing games on Fridays. This is how I taught my students to handle money. When I received an email from a friend telling me that my kindergarten teacher passed away, I was stunned. I will never forget how after she cleaned my uniform, she took my hands, and we started to mix the colors that were splattered on the table. Suddenly, I was watching how red, green, and yellow turned into a rainbow.

During the summer of 2006, I took a course in holistic education and urban issues. Rather than defining and analyzing the pejoratives of urban education, I took it as a dialectical process of contextualizing my practice as a teacher and researcher (Craig, 2000, 2006b). The experience, for me, meant to start engaging myself in a deep inquiry regarding education. I cannot forget the argument made by one of our classmates, who asserted that the disenfranchised are always at the bottom, regardless of the reforms that are made in education. Ho (2004) reminds us that, despite the legislation in place, the discrimination and displacement of the disabled student continues to be a common practice.

The social model of disabilities studies has provided us with the tools to conceptualize the social nature of impairment and disability. However, serious inquiry into the nature of special education in terms of empowerment continues to be absent. Moreover, while some disability scholars have condemned critical theorists and the social model, we continue to lack an emancipatory pedagogy for the disabled from the academy in general. Instead, these scholars provide a limiting and restrictive vision for the future of the disabled. Rather than devising avenues for providing a voice to the disabled, scholars such as Gabel continue to argue about the metaphoric construction of the term voice. My claim is that we need to move beyond that modality and proceed into the realm of what makes a liberating process for the disabled a reality.

My other claim is that special education might look different, once we start constructing and providing the spaces where the disabled student can start having a voice. Perhaps it is more important that such voices are taken into account within the contextual experience of the disabled. To put it bluntly, I do not believe that special education and disability studies have reached that point.

I conclude that the current educational system is designed to place the disabled into the most restrictive environment. My own experience is a testimony of an education of possibility in my early years, along with the pedagogy of restriction in my secondary education. Although I agree with Gabel (2002) that any pedagogy must be concerned with the safety of the students, I have to conclude that such concern for safety must not hinder the pedagogical experience of the disabled. My argument is that special education must be daring and bold enough to allow these students the freedom to explore their world. If we are to accept the notion that pedagogy is a human continuum, then we must accept the radical proposition that education involves humans between the end-points of teachers and students.

Proposing a liberatory pedagogy for the disabled causes me both excitement and fear. I am excited that there might be a way for us to intellectually forge the pedagogical possibilities for the disabled. I also believe that we can learn from countless examples where the disabled was allowed to fully experience his or her capacities, and envision a better future for millions of people. In contrast, I am fearful that the possibilities of liberation for the disabled might not yield the desired vision. Rather, I am afraid that my argument would unleash a series of arguments from those who are skeptical about the possibilities of a liberatory pedagogy for the disabled.

I do believe that critical pedagogy has the best promise for the emancipation of the disabled. I am confident that scholars are wise and educated enough to realize that critical pedagogues talk about oppression in the broadest of context. The omission of certain groups does not translate into a deficiency of the theory. Rather, I have faith that the example of liberation for one group (e.g., Freire's Brazilian peasants) can empower others to follow the example. It must also be remembered that the disabled have not been oppressed exclusively due to their impairment, but because of their racial, economical, and social entity (Ferri & Connor, 2005). Pedagogical scholars across the board need to address the fact that, at times, disability is only one component of oppression in the life of an impaired person.

The crucial questions, here, are whether a liberatory pedagogy for the disabled works, whether we can envision scenarios of liberation for the disabled, and whether a disability dictates to what extent that liberation is possible. This brings me to a personal challenge. I wonder what would have happened if, instead of climbing the tree, I would have abstained from doing it. As in critical pedagogy, pedagogy of the disabled is about taking risks (Freire, 1970/2000). I took a risk that day, and I want to believe that, on that day, I left behind the symbolic crutches that would have hindered me for the rest of my life.

THIRTEEN

MY INQUIRY

> I knew that when the great guiding spirit cleaves humanity into two antagonistic halves, I will be with the people.
>
> —Ernesto Ché Guevara, *The Motorcycle Diaries*

> Reason is only reason, and it only satisfies man's rational requirements. Desire, on the other hand, is the manifestation of life itself.
>
> —Fyodor Dostoyevsky, Notes from the Underground

The central theme of this work is that both the world of academia and that of everyday life need the agency of self-reflection and inquiry. As such, this project—originally developed as a discursive avenue—was provoked by reflecting upon my own location as a narrative inquirer in both the formal education/academic settings and those of my mundane life as a struggling special education teacher and disabled individual. It developed out of my own trajectory of self-reflection and the social conditions that enabled me to function within the existing frame of society. It also developed out of my existence within the institution of public education, which provokes me to be critical of the institution. It also developed from my personal life.

As my doctoral and teaching endeavor took place, and I became more involved in my work, I noticed that this would be a personal as much as a theoretical work. The personal reflects my need to investigate my social position as a disabled individual and a special education teacher. It grew out of my need to examine the life of the disabled in this postmodern capitalistic social culture, global society, and post 9/11 era. Without a doubt, this project represents my own self-reflection of the social educator who is seeking justice in the field of disability studies. This is a reflection of how my own life experience has shaped and organized my worldview and my practice (Britzman, 2003). Using an autobiographical approach widely used in narrative inquiry (Chan, 2006; Ross, 2003; Seaman, 2008), the stories reflected in this work are my own. In the end, this is my way of reconciling the pedagogy I seek and the pedagogy I have found.

The theoretical theme developed out of my need to make sense of the problems that I still find with special education. Despite what some claim that special education has made the disabled's life better, I think special education needs to fulfill the promise of a better education experience for millions of disabled students (Ferri & Connor, 2005; Fulton & Sabornie, 1994; Reiser, 2006a). The theoretical and academic component of this piece is more than just a mere quest for validity. It is a quest for the teacher as a curriculum maker (Craig, 2001, 2006b). As such, this is the acknowledgment that teaching is a very human experience, and that we cannot separate our human experiences once inside the classroom (Bruner, 1990). Secondly, as an academic paper, this work seeks those voices that explore the need for the full-lived curriculum (Aoki, 1989/1990). This work is also searching for the curriculum-as-lived, which acknowledges that what students bring to the classroom is just as valuable and important as what teachers have to share. At the very core, this is what I regard as a full-lived curriculum.

Narrative Inquiry: The Theoretical

The methodology I use is narrative inquiry (Connelly & Clandinin, 1990); it is as a research approach broadly used across many disciplines such as psychology (Bruner, 1990, 1993), religion (Crites, 1971), history (D. Carr, 1986), and disability studies (M. Carr, 1995; Hehir, 2005; Valentine, 2007). As Bruner explains (Bruner, 1991):

> [W]e organize our experience and our memory of human happenings mainly in the form of narrative—stories, excuses, myths, reasons for doing and not doing, and so on. Narrative is a conventional form, transmitted culturally and constrained by each individual's level of mastery and by his conglomerate of prosthetic devices, colleagues, and mentors. (p. 4)

For some scholars (Bruner, 1990; Dewey, 1938b), narrative is an essential characteristic of organizing personal knowledge and social experiences. For other scholars, narrative is the basic human characteristic of "a story-telling animal" (Craig, 2006b, p. 263), and of making "a dialogic interaction both with our surrounding world and with ourselves" (Moen, 2006, p. 2).

In education, narrative has been used extensively as an accepted form of research (i.e., Chan, 2006; Clandinin & Connelly, 1992; Conle, 2001; Connelly, Phillion, & He, 2003; Craig, 2001; McLaren, 1997; Moen, 2006; Olson & Craig, 2005; Tierney, 2002). As such, narrative inquiry has been used to understand the teacher as curriculum maker (Clandinin & Connelly, 1992; Craig, 2001; Ross, 2003), explore teachers' lives (Clandinin & Connelly, 1996), and validate their narratives as lived stories (Conle, 2000; Craig, 2006a).

Narrative inquiry broadly builds upon the legacy of John Dewey (Bruner, 1990; Connelly & Clandinin, 1999; Craig, 2006b). According to Bruner (1990), John Dewey saw language as an avenue for humans to sort out our thoughts and make clear our views about the world we live in. Language, in other words, is an essential tool that we use to express our ideas and feelings about our lives. For Dewey (1938b), language was very important in formulating "substantial meaning" in the field of inquiry (p. 77). The concept of looking at language as an agency for shaping our thoughts about the world and as a tool for making substantial meaning has serious implications for narrative inquiry. According to Dewey, "man is naturally a being that lives in association with others in communities possessing language, and therefore enjoying a transmitted culture" (Dewey, 1938b, p. 19). Narrative inquiry, therefore, becomes the agency to transmit culture, understand the views of the world, and analyze the way we make meaning about our lives.

However, the legacy of John Dewey in narrative inquiry is more than simply proposing language as the means to express our values and thoughts about the world. He saw education as an interactive process where education and life collided to project our human experiences. According to Dewey, "When we reflect upon an experience instead of just having it, we inevitably distinguish between our attitude and the objects toward which we sustain the attitude"

(Dewey, 1916/1944, p. 166). Inquiry is synonymous with a reflexive process, and, as human, we cannot help but be reflexive and ponder about our actions. Therefore, inquiry enters "into every area of life and into every aspect of every area" (Dewey, 1938b, p. 102). The result is that inquiry becomes the intimate act of looking at different affairs of our lives, and how those affairs play into our existence.

At the core, Dewey (1938a) asserts that we learn from experience. Therefore, inquiry is not just a mode of analyzing and deconstructing our actions. The essence of inquiry is to reflect upon what we have learned from experience and how that has transformed and changed us. All learning comes from "personal experience," according to Dewey, and he saw such learning as a genuine form of education (p. 25). This has significant consequences. Learning forces us to move inward and outward, backward and forward in our lives. We encounter and reflect upon the activities we enjoy, the pain that makes us suffer, and the experiences that ultimately make us grow (Craig, 2006b). It is important to note that for Dewey (1916/1944, 1938a, 1938b), learning, inquiry, and experience were intimately linked. By reflecting on the things upon which we act and the things which act upon us, humans move about their lives by "their own intelligence and ideas" (Dewey, 1908/1981, p. 16).

Finding the Teacher's Voice

Based upon the contribution of John Dewey, cotemporaries of narrative inquiry have thought to validate the teachers' voice (e.g., Bruner, 1990; Clandinin & Connelly, 1995; Connelly & Clandinin, 1990; Craig, 2006b; Ellis, 1997; Olson & Craig, 2005; Pinar, 1997; Tierney & Lincoln, 1997). For example, Connelly and Clandinin (1999) have used narrative inquiry to understand teachers as "knowers of themselves, of their situation, of children, of subject matter, of teaching, of learning" (p. 1). To capture the essence of teaching as an experience, Connelly and Clandinnin (1990) developed the term "personal practical knowledge" (p. 1). At its essence, this is a way "of reconstructing the past and the intention of the future with the exigencies of the present situation" (Connelly & Clandinin, 1988, p. 25). This form of narrative inquiry forces us to ponder about our past, see how that past shapes our present, and realize what the consequences are for the future. In other words, this bold statement indicates that what we are and what we do will be projected toward the future, and these actions are shaped by what we did and experienced in our lives. Perhaps it is important to assert that our actions are not separate. On the contrary, this is a stark revelation that our actions are the direct result of our experiences.

For Connelly and Clandinin, the act of acknowledging what we learn from experience could best be expressed through narrative:

> Increasingly, as our work progressed, we came to see teacher knowledge in terms of narrative as life history, as storied life composition. These stories, those narratives of experience, are both personal—reflecting a person's life history—and social—reflecting the milieu, the contexts in which teachers live. (Connelly & Clandinin, 1999, p. 2)

When inquiry becomes a narrative, it becomes a landscape in which the story becomes a lived agency. However, Connelly and Clandinin (1999) are keen in differentiating between the stories that take place within the school and the classroom. They stress the importance of noticing that within the school and within the classroom there are different stories taking place. Within those walls, there are "secret stories," "cover stories," and "sacred stories" taking place (Clandinin & Connelly, 1996; Crites, 1971). The stories of people—these lived stories (Craig, 2006b)—reflect the lives of the individual within a particular institution, making indispensable the notion that within a school's walls living experiences go on within thc formal and informal curriculum. What is imperative to notice is that within this way of thinking and approaching the stories of teachers and schools, important questions started to arise. These became questions of identity such as: "What is my story within the classroom, hallways, and school?

As narrative inquiry develops, the story of teachers and teachers stories within the classroom started to emerge (Aoki, 1989/1990; Chan, 2006; Craig, 2003, 2006a; Ross, 2003). Ted Aoki (1989/1990), while a phenomologist, not a narrative inquirer, has been instrumental in developing the notion that teachers are the curriculum makers. His metaphor of the half-lived curriculum is a powerful analogy that teachers and students are the ones that shape and make the curriculum. On the other hand, narrative has helped us understand teachers not as reform doers or mere knowledge dispensers, but as reform and knowledge makers (Craig, 2000, 2001). Recent contributions from Chan (2006) and Ross (2003) remind us that curriculum is not a piece of paper or a mere document it is, rather, the lived experiences that teachers and students live within and outside the classroom. Ross (2003) says it best when she defines curriculum as an "organic connection," which best represents the experiences that are lived within the four walls of the classroom (p. 569).

Narrative inquiry is about voice. William F. Pinar (1997) asserts that the teacher's voice is crucial. He states that:

> [V]oice has become crucial in portraying these calls to speak and teach. In the efforts to understand curriculum as political, racial, gender, phenomenological, and autobiographical text, voice has been elaborated and employed extensively. (p. 82)

However, what do we see when a voice becomes an effort to understand the curriculum socially, politically, culturally, and autobiographically? As such, voice becomes a process for breaking the silence (J. L. Miller, 1982) and finding oneself in it (Pinar, 1997). However, finding voice is an act of fear as much as it is an act of liberation. For example, Janet L. Miller wrote:

> The dream is recurring: the quiet everywhere. It surrounds my classroom, penetrates the halls of the building in which I teach. I wait for my students, for the voices, horrified that they might scream in rage, trembling that they may never whisper. (quoted in Pinar, 1997, p. 82)

In this instance, Miller shows us the fear of breaking the silence and the splitting of the teacher's spirit within the walls of education formality. Miller goes on and asks: "How much [does] it take to break the silence?" (quoted in Pinar, 1997, p. 82). Miller's answer is that breaking the silence "creates ways to ground my fears of unnatural silence and to focus my voice, my energies upon the articulation of our work together" (quoted in Pinar, 1997, p. 82). Despite the fears, the result of breaking the silence is liberating. It gives us the chance to find the spaces where we can truly free our spirits and our souls in order to truly understand the teacher/student human dynamic.

However, the question must be presented: What does narrative inquiry seek in voices? Miller (1990) asserts that voices bring teachers "to the center of the dialogue and debate surrounding current educational reforms, teacher education restructuring efforts, and research on teachers' knowledge" (p. 10). Deborah Britzman argues that voice "enables the individual to participate in a community" (quoted in Connelly & Clandinin, 1990, p. 4). It becomes clear that narrative inquiry seeks the need of the teacher to be heard and be part of the community. However, the need to seek a voice, whether of teachers or students, reaffirms that everyone is an active member of that community, and ultimately, we all have a say in shaping the outcome of the community. Britzman reminds us that "[f]inding the words, speaking for oneself, and feeling heard by others are all part of this process" (quoted in Pinar, 1997, p. 83).

FOURTEEN

SOCIAL VOICES

Narrative, as a form of voice, has also become a political tool for those who are the least heard (Kincheloe, 1997; McLaren, 1997, 2003b; Pinar, 1997). Voices in education have been silenced. Pinar (1997) affirms that voices provide the opportunity for those "marginalized in curriculum research" to be heard (p. 83). Britzman argues that voice is an essential part of an individual's social participation in a community (referenced in Pinar, 1997).

As a form of social justice, narrative has been used to validate teachers' and students' voices. McLaren (2003b) refers to the voices of teachers and students as a form of culture and knowledge. He states that "[a] student's voice is not a reflection of the works as much as it is a constitutive force that both mediates and shapes reality within historically constructed practices and relationships of power" (quoted in Pinar, 1997, p. 84). Additionally, McLaren explains that "[t]eacher's voice reflects the values, ideologies, and structuring principle that teachers use to understand and mediate the histories, cultures, and subjectivities of their students" (quoted in Pinar, 1997, p. 84).

Within this context, voice is not a narration for mere storytelling sake. Pinar (1997) explains that voice is a dual social act of stories that teachers and students tell each other, so they can construct a bigger picture. This becomes an attempt to tear down the walls of hegemony and power in education as teachers and students become unified participants in the pedagogic process, compelling them to teach and learn from each other (McLaren, 2003b).

Narrative, as a form of social justice, has become a tool for criticizing the orthodoxy of the educational institution. Pinar (1997) argues that formal "scholarship and research are rhetorical, implicated in the institutions, with their own self-serving and competitive cultures" (p. 93). Steinberg and Kincheloe (quoted in Pinar, 1997) have fostered the creation of a post-formal thinking in education where there is an end to the white-male experience in life in "which all other experiences are measured" within the institution (p. 90). Within the post-formal thinking, Shirley R. Steinberg and Joe L. Kincheloe (quoted in Pinar, 1997) offer a curriculum where the truths are uncovered, discovered, and revealed, helping us understand our realities and our relationships to power from plural perspectives. As a critique for the institution of education, narrative as a social justice is significant because it can shake education's undisturbed foundation.

In the academic setting, narrative can be personal. Ellis (1997) observes that academic discourse "camouflages the 'I'—the writer herself acting and feeling" (p. 116). In her response to the academic discourse that camouflages the "I," Ellis (1997, 2002, 2004) advocates for a more personal and emotional form of narrative, insisting that in evocative and passionate narrative is where she finds insight and comfort.

We might be compelled to argue that Ellis only seeks a narrative that is emotional and evocative for the sake of being emotional and evocative; however, her desire is also to promote the narrative of social change. For Ellis (2002), the "personal is political" as much as the "political is personal" (p. 403), and she argues that for quite some time social activism has concentrated itself in the abstract and rhetorical, avoiding a more personal stance. Her stance is, however, that there is a "growing recognition of the important connections among narrative, autoethnography, social activism, and social practice" (Ellis, 2002, p. 403). Ellis (2002), in her defense, asserts that narrative is the missing link between abstract theory of the academy and those advocating for social change. Narrative must foster social change, which means "to write from the heart, touch other people, or improve social conditions" (Ellis, 1997, p. 135).

The Self-Reflective Act

Narrative, as a form of inquiry, starts with the notion that we, as humans, are living organisms that "lead storied lives" (Connelly & Clandinin, 1990, p. 2). Narrative, then, is a self-reflective process which builds on the professional experience of the researcher (Chan, 2006; Ross, 2003). This project is a self-reflection of my professional landscape knowledge. Narrative inquiry, as a form of research, is a report of history, whether it is the history of the research, the researcher, or the researched. This is what Polkinghorne (1997) defines as a "motion picture depicting the process as it happened" (p. 15). Narrative becomes, as a result, the recollection of past episodes. As a reflective process, as Polkinghorne (1997) describes, narrative brings full meaning to an experience, enhancing the understanding of an event. The narrative process, as described above, is not simply the recollection of events as it happened, but the self-reflection of emotions, values, feelings, ideals, and physical and bodily demonstrations that makes the process meaningful and the experience worthwhile (Ellis, 1997; Polkinghorne, 1997). It is an evocative act in which the innermost corners of our souls are explored in search of how our experiences have affected and changed us.

It should come, therefore, as no surprise that narrative inquiry has become a personal endeavor for researchers to find their own voice in which they can talk about "what mattered to them in the stories to live by" (Connelly & Clandinin, 1990, p. 4). For example, Ted Aoki (1983) brilliantly narrates his experience as a Japanese Canadian growing up in the midst of World War II, and he explains how this experience shaped his life as a teacher, a father who lost his daughter, and an individual who in Japan was perceived as a foreigner and Canadian, despite his Japanese ancestry. Vicki Ross (2003) wrote about how her personal views shaped her way of interacting with the math curriculum, and, ultimately, narrates her approach to her research as a doctoral student. Carolyn Ellis (1997, 2003) has written extensively about her personal experiences with fear, growth, and personal loss. In all these examples, and in many others (e.g., M. Carr, 1995; Rose, 1997; Whelan, 1997), we see that narrative inquiry is no longer a methodology that uses the distant observer and the observed. Rather, narrative inquiry becomes a personal quest for understanding our own personal experience as researchers, observers, and protagonists.

What becomes clear is that narrative is the process of learning about us in certain cultural settings. However, narrative is also a powerful and emotionally charged tool. Ellis (1997, 2004) has used narrative to understand the loss of her husband, her college lover, and her brother, and to make sense of her life during and after the terrorist attacks of 9/11. Muncey (2005) used narrative to explain such painful life episodes as sexual abuse or growing up poor.

Narrative inquiry as a self-reflective exercise has significant results. For McLaren (1997), "critical reflection" forges decisive thinking about the social structures of our lives (p. 170). In other words, the inquirer becomes aware of the transcendental effects of one's actions. This is what narrative inquiry is about. It means understanding what we have lived and how that lived story shapes our lives (Connelly & Clandinin, 1988). Ultimately, it is how we understand our experience in society. It means taking a closer look at who we are, where we are, where we came from, and where we are heading.

I am using narrative to synthesize my feelings, emotions, values, ideals, and physical and bodily demonstrations to explore how my life as a teacher and a disabled individual has affected me. Narrative as a self-reflective act is about connecting voices (Ellis, 1997). In using narrative as an exploration tool, I am connecting the voices of my past to understand my present and my future. These are the voices helping me understand who I am. This exercise, therefore, connects one's work to the rest of one's life (Ellis, 1997), which inevitably becomes a personal act.

Narrative Inquiry: The Personal

By using narrative inquiry, I will contextualize how the data will be presented, and I will interpret the spiritual transformation that occurred within my life. Such spiritual transformation only occurred after I delved into deep reflections and analysis through ad hoc methods such as journals, diaries, emails, letters, and conversations with others. This transformation also came about after realizing my place inside the classroom and society (McLaren, 2003b). In this framework, the data that I present is the retelling of my experiences and the spiritual changes that took place within me (Ellis, 1997).

I derive my narrative mainly from three schools of theory. The first theory is the notion of using narrative inquiry as an evocative and passionate process. Although it is often through the retelling of our stories that we can make sense of our lives, I believe that it is more important to dive into the emotions and feelings that experiences bring to us, which ultimately make us who we are (Ellis, 1997). The second theoretical foundation I use is moral education (R. Miller, 1990/1997; Purpel & McLaurin, 2004). I believe that such evocative transformation is the result of confronting such serious moral questions regarding public education: What do we really want to happen inside the classroom? What is the real purpose of special education? Whose interest does special education satisfy? The third theory that I use in my narrative is critical pedagogy. It is my belief that a pivotal pillar of my inner transformation is the capability of seeing education as an agent of the capitalistic and market-driven forces of society, which helps me understand the demand of the system to prepare students for a vocational career in the field of special education.

FIFTEEN

MY NARRATIVE

My narrative is guided by emerging questions that evolved during my years as a doctoral student, as I was exposed to moral education and critical pedagogy. During my early years as a doctoral student, I encountered the readings of Peter McLaren, Henry Giroux, Maxine Greene, David Purpel, and Joe Kincheloe, to name a few. Their critical analysis and view of education deeply influenced my own views. Their critical questioning of the current state of affairs of education revived my own fervor to critically question the institution as well. Suddenly, I started to see the evasion of critical social, cultural, political, and economical discourses in general education (Purpel & McLaurin, 2004), and how this discourse was also absent in special education (Valentine, 2007). As in general education, I also saw the stress on the technical—such as testing, tracking, and merit pay—rather than an emphasis on social, political, and moral issues (see Purpel & McLaurin, 2004, p. 19).

This extraordinary chasm between the trivialized discourse in special education (e.g., inclusion vs. exclusion, teachers' training, testing, parent advocacy, and so on) and more serious moral questions regarding education and disability helps me to frame two basic questions: How can we continue to explain the continuing phenomenon of trivializing the special education discourse in light of the crucial issues of our times? Second, what would constitute a proper point of departure for a more serious conversation in special education? With these two basic questions in mind, other questions also started to emerge. For example, I started to wonder whether or not special education is really working for the disabled. And if the answer was yes, whose needs and agendas are truly being met in special education? Why do we continue to view special education as if it were a totally separate field from general education?

The evolution of such questions comes from different places. On one hand, such questions come from society's never-ending love affair of placing, characterizing, and labeling individuals by race, gender, socio-economic status, and disability. It also evolved from the continuing process of using the labels "disabled" and "normal" interchangeably as if "normality" is something that can truly be achieved. Additionally, these questions emerged from the dehumanizing and marginalizing treatment that disabled people have received for years. Moreover, this came about from critically analyzing the field of special education, realizing that special education is a field that still needs to achieve a concise discourse on liberatory pedagogy. Furthermore, such questions evolved out my own belief that, like the rest of the education field (Purpel & McLaurin 2004), those of us working with the disabled in public education are still dazed and confused about what we want to achieve and how to go about achieving it.

Like the rest of the scholars of disabilities (Blanchet, Brantlinger, & Shealey, 2005; M. Carr, 1995; Edgar, 1997; Gabel, 2002; Gallagher, 1995; Howe & Miramontes, 1991; Kauffman & Hallahan, 1995), I also have questions regarding special education. Like many others, I wonder if the system is truly working for the disabled, wrestling with the question of whether or not inclusion is the best avenue (Gabel, 2002). However, I have other questions too, such as: Are we taking the time and the energy to really define what we want special education to be? Are we asking ourselves what special education is for? Are we really figuring out what would constitute a valuable learning experience for the disabled? With the passing of time, I was more intrigued by analyzing the educational experiences of the disabled rather than focusing my argument on more technical questions about whether or not special education was working, and these questions helped me find that path.

I knew that these were not easy questions, and I knew that it would require an immense amount of energy to find the answers. However, I knew that these questions were also intimately related to me: Did special education work for me as a student? Is it working for me as a professional? How do I see myself within this profession? With these questions, I started to question what would constitute a valuable educational experience for the disabled; however, as time passed, I realized that such questions would become personal. As my doctoral research progressed, I saw myself from new and different angles. I questioned my pedagogy as a teacher, wondering whether I was the liberating teacher that I wanted to be.

This narrative takes a fluid path as an experience which redirects itself many times (Seaman, 2006), and it is within this fluid reflection that I intend to recollect my thoughts about my experience. What does this story tell us? How do I intend to move forward? How do I expect my journey to contribute to the larger community? By analyzing my experience as an educator, these are some of the questions that I plan to answer. In the end, I intend to reflect upon the spiritual transformation that my journey has produced in me.

My task is not easy. As a work in progress, I know that I have many ways of expressing my experience. However, I chose a different route. Rather than examining better ways to teach, I pursued the conscious act of exploring the state of being, and I immersed myself in the world of a the teacher as an active being trying to find a liberating pedagogy and an emancipatory praxis for my students. I could not agree with Valentine (2007) more when he states how colleges and universities only indoctrinate teachers to be technicians or banking educators (Freire, 1970). Therefore, this is why I am departing from the attractive notion of imparting a remedy to a problem. Rather, I nurture the possibility of engaging myself in my multiple roles within the profession of special education. I am taking the challenge of a praxis that requires me to understand myself as a teacher and disabled individual with the tensions, pains, and gratifications that this exercise may produce.

My narrative raises the issue of being. It is an ontological exercise of crafting my experiences in the hope that I can move toward a better definition of what it takes to live as a disabled individual and be a special education teacher. It also investigates how the mundane experiences in the school trenches help us, as human beings, define our world, space, and landscape. In this sense, my particular role in this narrative is to understand how those experiences helped me move toward a better view of myself. As before, new, exciting, and intriguing questions started to emerge: What helped me move forward and backward? What holds me back? What has helped me to transgress?

Despite my temptations, it is not my goal to write "how to go about" liberating students as a role of the special education teacher. My biggest hope, within this narrative, is to clarify our need to do it.

SIXTEEN

SUBJECT MATTER AND MILIEU

The only journey is the one within.

—Rainer Maria Rijke

I have but one lamp by which my feet are guided, and that is the lamp of experience. I know no way of judging of the future but by the past.

—Edward Gibbon

This chapter is the retelling of my personal experience lived as a disabled individual, teacher, doctoral student, and immigrant, believing that these different facets of my life function as one. I borrow from Schwab (1973) that we cannot omit the experiences that we live as teachers and learners through the milieu and the subject matter. Furthermore, Schwab (1971) tells us that we cannot learn what to teach from teaching and learning alone, and we also learn to teach from particular circumstances of the time, the place, and the person. This only tells me that every action in our lives as teachers is shaped by who we are, where we come from, and what we have experienced. The experience of teaching does not occur in a vacuum.

However, I believe that narrative, for narrative's sake, only serves a very shallow purpose. Narrative should be an evocative action allowing us to explore what we are ready to learn about ourselves and the world around us (Ellis, 1997). This chapter is more than the mere retelling of my personal stories. It is an exercise, which will help me to learn about myself and the world around me.

I have the firm belief that my life as a disabled student, teacher, doctoral student, and critical pedagogue did not occur in isolated spaces. They are all integral parts of who I am as a whole. Before I begin the retelling of my story, it is important to build a concise theoretical framework in which my story is based: teacher/learner, subject matter, and milieu. I borrow this theoretical framework from

Schwab (1973) and Seaman (2007) as the guide that can put order to my thoughts, providing the reader with an orderly account of my experience.

Teacher/Learner

As I begin the narration of my life, I understand that there is a commonplace in my life, which identifies me as a learner and a teacher. While I always understood my role as a teacher, and as my teaching profession started, I realized that the students in my classroom were also my teachers. As my teaching experience progressed, I understood the classroom as an environment with learning and teaching experiences. This is the concept of seeing the teacher as a learner, borrowed from Seaman (2008), which takes into consideration that education is more than the mere dispensing of knowledge by the teacher. This is the framework that fully takes into account that teaching is a lifelong learning experience, which often teacher training does not take into account (Clandinin & Connelly, 1994).

I agree with Seaman (2008) that defining the teacher as learner is an easy task. However, if the act of learning takes into account more than a single variable within the classroom and explores the kaleidoscope of emotions, feelings, memories, experiences, and situations within a particular classroom, then the task becomes complicated. This is why it is my belief that teachers do not solely teach but also learn. Therefore, this study, as an autobiographical inquiry, is not only a reflection of stories I tell the reader, but the examination of stories I tell myself and what I am ready to learn from the stories and the retelling (Ellis, 1997). I agree with Clandinin and Connelly (1994), furthermore, that teachers not only learn to be teachers from the classroom but from life as well. As Craig (1995) reminds us, there is no such a thing as the abstract world of the classroom, but the classroom interacts with every other aspect of the world and of our lives.

Subject Matter

As I stepped into my classroom for the very first time, I knew that this was not ordinary teaching, and the students knew that as well. I was not only a teacher, but I was also a student by night. However, I was no ordinary teacher for my students. I was a disabled teacher, which was a totally different experience for many of them. I knew that they would learn something from me, and I was ready to learn something from them. I knew that what they brought with them was just as valuable to me as what I was offering them.

The subject matter could easily be defined as my classroom experiences. Nevertheless, in a self-study where emotions and experiences are evoked, this task becomes more complicated. The subject matter is not only what I learned in my teaching pre-service classes and my daily life as a teacher; it is what I carried all my life as a special education student, a doctoral student immersed in critical and moral education theory, and as a disabled individual.

The term "subject matter" in a narrative can have many meanings. Within this project, it is my own personal experiences. These are my experiences as a disabled student in three different countries from my kindergarten days in Argentina to my days as a doctoral student as an adult at University of Houston. While the main subject matter of this project is to envision a moral perspective on disability and education, I cannot detach myself from my previous experiences that contributed to my own personal view of the world. The context in which I bring the subject matter in this project is not only restricted to what I teach in the classroom, but also to my personal aspirations of what I envision in the field of special education. As such, the goal of this narrative-inquiry is to provide a clearer personal vision of special education through a better understanding of myself. It is important for me to not only look at my experience as a teacher, but also to revive my experience as a former student who also received disability services. This is what will emerge from my narrative.

Milieu

The final piece of my inquiry is the milieu, or the context, of my narrative. Seaman (2008) reminds us that all narratives are told within certain sets of circumstances. While depending on the situation and the experiences, my milieu changes, and the context of this self-study focuses on the vision of special education provided by my experiences.

This inquiry started with my involvement with the Social Education Department at the College of Education at the University of Houston. I believe that it was then that I developed my current vision of education. My first class in social education was a social studies method class taught by Dr. Tony Talbert in the fall of 2001. My initial image of the class was that I was going to learn how to do lesson plans, revise the curriculum, and analyze the ways in which social studies was properly taught. Nothing could have been further from the truth. Dr. Talbert immediately made the distinction between the social studies class as we know it, where the teacher lectures and hands out worksheets, and what social studies should be. In his class, we devised alternative ways of teaching social studies through games, activities such as the box exercise, the experience of museums, and the need to make history relevant to today's issues. In the wake of the tragic episodes of 9/11, which occurred only three weeks after class started, the significance of Dr. Talbert's class became more important to me than ever before. The challenge of looking at social studies differently from what I was used to left me with the hunger for more. That was when I decided to continue with social education.

The next spring I decided to enroll in the second social studies method class taught by my current advisor and friend, Dr. Cameron White. I barely knew anybody in Social Education, so I did not know what to expect. I desperately wanted someone to tell me more conventional ways of teaching social studies. However, once more, I was challenged to rethink what social studies was all about. The very first book that I read in Dr. White's class was *Lies My Teacher Told Me* by James Loewen (1995). The book properly depicts all the erroneous and false facts that the average U.S. History textbook contains. The weekly roundtable discussions about the book opened my eyes like never before. It was after this class that I knew I would never see social studies and education in the same light again.

I became a full-time teacher at a high school in Northwest Houston in the fall of 2004, a year after I became a doctoral student. Already groomed in the Social Education vision of public schools, I was looking at education in a different light. However, I was not sure of which path to take. I was immersed in the activities and the academic life of social education. In the spring of 2005, I went to Montreal for a conference. The opportunity to listen to different academicians about the possibility of social justice in the classroom opened my mind about what to do. While walking on the grounds of McGill University with Dr. Jason Apodaca, the idea of writing a dissertation about my personal experience as a disabled teacher in special education surfaced. When I got back to Houston, I was ready to write.

SEVENTEEN

THE FIELD WITH THE MANGO TREES

Venezuela was so different from Argentina. All I remember seeing from the airplane's window was this extremely thick forest, a lake, and a chain of islands appearing though the clouds. It reminded me of that scene in King Kong when the ship approaches the mysterious island through the fog. From the airplane's window, I saw this long canal ending in a gigantic pool of water. Ships were traveling the canal in all directions, and I saw these towers one after the other, like the towers where dad worked in the Patagonian field, only they were in the water. Rain poured from the sky as if the heavens were weeping with no end in sight. When I stepped out, my breath was taken away. It felt as if I had hit an invisible wall of water. The air was no longer cool and crisp, but heavy, dense and moist. In a matter of thirty minutes or so, I was drenched in my own sweat as we waited in the customs terminal. The land was no longer barren, desert-like, and desolate, but it had this thick and dark vegetation. Something inside of me said I was not going to see snow for a very long time. Deep in my heart, I knew that the constant wind gusts and the winter storms would become distant memories from the past.

With the exception of my family and other people that came with us in the plane, people were darker-skinned, speaking a different and more accelerated Spanish with a different accent; some would speak English, and yet others were speaking Dutch or German. I remember I was hungry. For the first time in my life, I ate a cheeseburger with a shake and fries.

My new bedroom was weird and it had no radiator by the window. I felt uncomfortable as my mom tucked me into bed that night. I slept covered with a single sheet. I was no longer bundled in three layers of blankets like before. "You won't be bundled like an Eskimo anymore," she said. There was a fan spinning on the ceiling, and I was afraid it would fall onto my bed. I remember feeling the wind the ceiling fan generated though the sheets, which made me uncomfortable. I always liked to bundle up when I slept. I woke the next morning and the window was open with the sounds of birds and a fresh breeze coming through. All I remember was my dad saying, "Breakfast is ready." I asked for croissants (we used to call them "half-moons") or Danish pastry. The maid serving breakfast smiled and said, "Half . . . what?" I ate fruit and drank orange juice for breakfast for the very first time in my life.

After breakfast, I stepped outside. The house melted with the outside world as doors and windows were wide open for the air to flow. Dad no longer wore his long thick overalls and parkas on his way to work. Mom no longer wore her wool sweaters and wool pants with her leather boots. Everyone was wearing a single layer of very light clothing and sandals, even mom, which made me feel weird. Sandals were only for the beach. I felt naked at first. Mom gave me a pair of shorts and put them on me. "Here," she said, "people wear this year round." The phone rang. It was Grandma. Mom's eyes became red and watery suddenly. She said very softly, "I really miss you, too."

I remember hearing shouting, laughing and cheering coming from outside. I went to look. Boys and girls of all ages were gathering in an empty field across the street from my house. Most of them were standing under a giant mango tree. I thought they were playing football (soccer) but they were not. There must have been at least forty of them. A tall, blond girl was trying to hit a small, brown ball with a flat, long paddle. She was facing the other way from three sticks buried in the ground, while a boy a distance away from the girl threw the brown ball. The girl hit the ball with the big paddle. The ball flew in the air and another boy caught it before it hit the ground. Half of the crowd shouted in disappointment and the other half shouted in joy. They played in the field all day long past sunset. They did this regularly.

How can I forget those days? The smell of rotten mangoes on the ground is as fresh today as it was twenty-nine years ago. We would go home at noon, have lunch, do our homework as fast as we could, and head for the field. Fighting and arguing would start right away. After all, we all wanted to play with the best. Being on the same team with Angel, Raj, Pablo, Kevin or Sandro would be almost a guaranteed victory. Daniel would always pitch for us. Freddy, my brother, would be in the outfield. Somewhere around three or four in the afternoon, my older sisters with their high school friends would arrive to put order into an almost chaotic scene of yelling and arguing. After much debate, we would start playing our own bastardized version of street baseball. Rules were made on the go, like in the best version of a street game. As the scorching Venezuelan sun burned our faces and the humidity took our breath away, we would start playing. One more time, we would spend another afternoon in the field with the mango trees.

The Meaning of the Field

Over the years, the field with the mango trees became an ever-powerful force in my life. This was an empty field across the street from my house in the international oil compound where we lived in Venezuela. This was where Brits, Canadians, Trinidarians, Argentines, Americans, Chileans, Brazilians, and scores of others would gather to play every afternoon, whether it was baseball, soccer, or any other sport. Metaphorically, the field represents who I am as a human being: an Argentine who left his hometown when I was only four, went back for a year at the age of six, and left for good when I was seven. It represents the place where, over the years, I would confront the Argentine and the non-Argentine in me. It represents the place where I would meet some of the most important people in my life, and who, over the years, became the extended family I never knew.

In the literal sense, the field represents the place where we had so much fun, where friendships were made that would last a lifetime, where rivalries were forged, where love and romance were found and broken, and where the sunset would be the silent witness of young people enjoying the prime of their lives. The field with mango trees is the symbol of who I am as a person, as a disabled, as a non-disabled, as a teacher, as a scholar, and as a human being. The field is the life that I left behind, the life I have in the present time, and the life that is ahead of me.

We all have that unique place in our life that defines who we are: that school, that neighborhood, that street, that classroom, that city, and for me, it is that field with mango trees under the caress of the scorching Venezuelan sun. In that sense, the field represents my life.

EIGHTEEN

THE DISABLED IN ME

As I explained before, I was born with cerebral palsy partly due to medical negligence and an accident that my mother had while she was pregnant. The experience of having a disability has produced mixed feelings within me. Yes, I wonder how people look at me. I wonder what they think when they hear me talk, watch me walk, and so on. I wonder what they feel about my presence. Like any other disabled person, I get frustrated. I remember this summer when I went to a baseball game in Boston with my friends from the UH grant in late June. I was amazed. I was finally at Fenway Park, home of the Boston Red Sox. However, the park is a century old. Our seats were high in the stands. I needed help to go up where there were no longer handrails to hold on to. As I sat in the stands, I wondered how I was going to get down when the game was over. I wondered why I could not go up and down the stairs as other people did to get a simple drink and a hot dog. I wondered what other people in my group were thinking. We had fun. We laughed. We cheered. Suddenly, I was having the time of my life. However, the thought never left me that particular evening.

The mango field, like Fenway Park, reminded me that my disability is only physical. Over the years, it is not how disabled I perceive myself to be that has influenced my view, but the possibility of living a full life. I have been fortunate to have a family and a close circle of friends who have always supported me. However, there is no doubt that my disability has greatly impacted my view of life. As a doctoral student, my thoughts are that anything in life is possible. However, what about the fact that I could never run fast? What would happen if I wanted to be a football player? What would happen if I wanted to be a soldier? Impossible dreams for somebody like me. Right? Perhaps. Nevertheless, my life experience has always taught me not to dwell on what I cannot do, but on what I can. As a teacher, this is the message that I want to send to my students.

For years, I never thought of the disabled in me. I went to college and got two degrees. I always worked, and I have always been fortunate to financially support myself. I became a teacher. However, it was in my classroom, as a teacher, that the disability image resurfaced. Students and parents were uneasy. I remember one student commenting about the fact that I was disabled. She said that teachers were not supposed to be disabled; they were not supposed to talk funny. One parent told me that she never returned my phone calls because she thought it was a drunk leaving a message. Painful thoughts, if you ask me.

As I walk with a cane again, due to an accident in late May, I wonder what has made me disabled and un-disabled. The things that have made me disabled, without a doubt, are my physical limitations. Nevertheless, I prefer to see myself more as an un-disabled person. Perhaps that is why I cannot see my students' limitations. Somewhere along the line, I was taught that I could, and that is how I see my students. That is what I want to show my students. However, where I am right now has come with great effort and sacrifices. It was not easy, as I will narrate in the following pages.

My Early Years

As a student, I was educated in three different countries: the United States, Argentina, and Venezuela. In all these places, my experiences were unique. In Argentina, I attended kindergarten, first, and second grade. In Venezuela, I attended school from third to seventh grade. In the United States, I attended school from eighth grade to graduate school.

The best word that I can use to describe my educational experience in Argentina is "motherly." There is not much that I can recall about what school was like on a daily basis. My only recollection from those years is how much Mrs. Torrecilla acted like a true mom to all of us. School was fun. We played in the playground, we visited the Railroad Museum, and we went to the beach. We were constantly recreating plays about national festivities. Perhaps it was the way my teachers were toward all of us that kept several of us in contact with them until they passed away. In an era when elementary school teachers are, for most, part of a distant memory, Mrs. Torrecilla became a lifelong friend and second mothers to so many of us.

In 1978, my family moved to Venezuela. The multi-national oil company, where my dad works to this day, sent us there for five years. I have mixed feelings about my experience in Venezuela. We had so much fun every afternoon in the field. Nevertheless, things got complicated in the classroom. Teachers were not willing to accommodate me. I was expected to do the normal work like everyone else. Even though I made the grade, things were difficult for me. Some teachers did not hide their resentment of having a disabled student in their classroom, and they made it clear they were not willing to help. In 1983, my dad decided to take a job offer in the United States. The main reason was that in the United States laws existed that protected the disabled student.

The field, as I explained before, was the place where we gathered every afternoon to play. This was the place where I was truly free. I played like everyone else, I ran like everyone else, and I was part of the team like everyone else. In the course of my life, bonds were forged in that field, which still last today. We were immigrants from all over the world, living thousands of miles away from our real relatives. In the scorching Venezuelan sun, we were becoming a family of our own. Over the years, this family has supported me in my struggles. These are the people that have told me I can, when sometimes I am the first one to say I cannot. These are the people that have shown me the un-disabled within me. We left Venezuela in 1983. The field no longer exists; a house was built on it, but I will never forget my life in the field and what that field meant to me.

Houston

In the fall of 1983, we arrived in Houston. I was immediately enrolled in eighth grade at Bleyl Junior High School, known today as Bleyl Middle School. For the first time since Argentina, the majority of my teachers were helping me with my work again. Ms. Zamora, the ESL teacher, would make me stay after school every day to supervise my homework. Ms. Nelson, the history teacher, would also help me. I remember that the assignments were easy. I was constantly making

A's. Bleyl, and in many ways, it reminded me of Argentina. Teachers were genuinely concerned about me again. Ms. Pogue, the Spanish teacher, constantly watched over me, as she seemed to be overly concerned about my safety in the hallways. Things were good at Bleyl. The only thing that bothered me was the regular schedule of seven classes every day, rather than the college-like schedule I was used to in Venezuela, where students take an average of 20 hours of instruction a week with plenty of playtime between classes. The seven hours bell-to-bell schedule was horrendous for me.

Cypress Creek, my high school, was very similar to Bleyl. Things were normal. Classes, transparencies, teachers talking the whole period, and the bell-to-bell schedule were the norm. However, as I matured, Cy-Creek, as we called it, was becoming a depressing place for me. Since I was very young, I wanted to do drafting and become either an architect or engineer. My counselor and my diagnostician, however, kept me in resource level or low-level classes for the entire four years I attended high school. They were extremely wary of placing me in more challenging classes. I was never allowed to take anything above Geometry. When I passed Geometry with an A, I was placed in resource consumer math regardless of the grade I earned. The only regular level classes I was allowed to take were in social studies. When I graduated, my high school academic transcript was worthless. I needed to do everything again at a local junior college for two years.

However, it is my relationship with Ms. Gallini from Cy-Creek, which impacted me the most. Contrary to other students, I was kept in a freshmen level study skills class with Ms. Gallini, now Mrs. De Boer, for the entire four years. My counselor, Mr. Matthews, thought that I needed the help. Ms. Gallini was a lady with whom I would develop a love and hate relationship. She was my tracking teacher, and the biggest discourager of allowing me to take drafting during high school. On the one hand, she discouraged me from even thinking about attending college. She said that people like me could be successful without attending college. I could always work with the Salvation Army or Goodwill. According to Ms. Gallini, those were the good jobs for the disabled, as she once said. On the other hand, she was my bigger supporter during my senior year. She was also the only teacher with whom I could openly share my frustrations. Over the course of the four years, we often argued about that fact that I wanted to be an architect. In a fit of rage, one day I walked out of her class, slamming the door shut. Ironically, after I graduated, she was my greatest cheerleader when it came to my dreams of becoming an architect.

NINETEEN

THE EARLY DAYS

When you come from a family of diplomats, engineers, doctors, university professors, and lawyers, the word teacher is a four-letter word. I was supposed to become an architect, and that was what I did. I graduated with an architecture degree in the spring of 1997. However, things never went well with architecture. I lost my will and my interest somewhere along the way, despite my initial fervor to become an architect, what started really well ended horribly wrong. From the top five percent of my class, I ended up on academic probation on my junior year. Right before graduation, my final presentation went extremely wrong. I made a fool of myself in front of the best of the best in the architecture world in Houston. Something was not ringing right. Since my junior year, something was not making sense to me anymore. I did manage to graduate from architecture school. However, my reputation as one of the most promising students in the architecture school was ruined.

After graduation, things were not going well either. I refused to take the critical computer design classes I needed to polish my skills. My portfolio was not good at all. Landing a job was something next to impossible. Believing that my architecture degree was worthless, I decided to enroll in the civil engineering program and stay in school. In the meantime, I kept my part-time job in the supermarket where I worked since a teenager. It was so ironic, an architecture graduate sacking groceries for a living. However, by that time, I was tired of surviving on minimum wage. Desperate about what to do, I followed the recommendations of a friend. I became a substitute teacher. The pay was more than the minimum wage that I was earning at the store. Substitute teaching also gave me the flexibility to work only a couple of days a week, while attending daytime classes. I kept my supermarket job only on the weekends. My seniority at the store assured me full-time status during the summer.

By the summer of 2003, I was desperate for a full-time job. I often talked to Mrs. Potter, the store general manager, about becoming a store manager. The pay was great, $55,000 a year to start. Working for Kroger since 1989, I knew the store like the back of my hand. I did everything from sacking groceries to closing the store by myself in the evening. However, Mrs. Potter always said that my future was not at Kroger. She had no doubt that I would become a great manager; however, she said I would be very unhappy. She recommended that I keep substitute teaching and only work at the store on the weekends. She had faith that I would get that teaching job. In the end, I would work at the store on the weekends until 2006, two years after I became a full-time teacher. For such a long time, Kroger was my home, even after I became a full-time teacher and a doctoral student attending conferences.

The Early Days

It is four thirty in the morning. My stomach is full of butterflies. I already drank my fifth or sixth cup of coffee while doing my calculus homework for engineering. I did not go to sleep at all. I was too nervous. It is a Monday, November 1999, and I am anxiously waiting for the phone to ring at five in the morning for my first substitute teaching assignment. In my mind, I was only thinking that I was going to finally earn in a week what I earned in a month at the store. The phone rang, and I took my first substitute assignment at my former high school, Cy-Creek. Things went pretty well, considering the fact that I substituted for an advanced placement history class, and that half of the students were, ironically, kids that worked with me at the store. The second assignment was at my former middle school, Bleyl. However, my third assignment would mark my fate; it was at the high school where I currently teach, which the name of I cannot mention at the request of the administration. I would never substitute anywhere else in the district.

As the days, months, and years went by, I gained a reputation as a good substitute teacher and somebody who got the job done. That assured me regular jobs at the school. I would substitute three days a week while I attended engineering classes twice a week. In the spring of 2000, after the finals were over, I was assigned to finish the year for a history teacher who literally walked out of the job on the middle of the day. At that time, the class was part of a pilot program where a history, math, English, and a science teacher would teach a joint curriculum as a team. The experience was wonderful and my team was very welcoming. The students were very receptive, and we finished the year with only one student failing the class. That assignment assured me permanent assignments to the point where teachers were requesting my services. Never in my wildest dreams had I thought that this was the beginning of my teaching career. On the last day of school, when we got out for the summer, I was on my way to my university to drop out of engineering and register in the teaching certification program. There was a change of heart occurring within me. I started to enjoy the schools and what I was experiencing inside the classrooms. I desperately wanted to be part of that. Suddenly, architecture became a long forgotten memory.

Certification: Social Ed, the Beginning

In the summer of 2000, I registered to become a certified teacher in history. In the beginning, things did not appear to have much excitement. I decided to finish the thirteen hours of history classes that I needed. My history minor was not enough. However, the history classes unleashed my appetite to learn more about social issues. I took a little bit of everything, from Islamic history to diplomacy to the CIA in the Middle East. Suddenly, I find myself avidly reading history, watching the news, and reading the newspapers on a daily basis. When I finished taking the hours for the history courses, I just simply kept taking more classes for the fun of it.

In the fall of 2001, I started to take education courses. In the beginning, they were the standard curriculum courses one takes in education. However, one of the courses was not the standard course as usual. I enrolled in Dr. Tony Talbert's secondary social studies methods class. From the beginning, Dr. Talbert's approach and vision of social studies influenced me. By then, I had been substituting for more than a year, so I knew that the average social studies class was nothing more than worksheets, reviews, transparencies, and tests. What happened to the fun in social education in the form of a recreated battle on the football field, the museums trips, and the costumed plays? I remember that Dr. Talbert invited a former student of his, who taught at a high school in the inner city. This teacher told us that every time he taught slavery, he dressed like a white Southerner, who walked with a cane. Suddenly, there was another way of teaching social studies.

In the spring of 2002, I enrolled in Dr. Cameron White's class, the second half of social studies methods. Honestly, I do not remember much of what I learned in terms of the specifics of what to do in the classroom. However, I remember that, at that particular moment, I wanted to become part of the Social Education program, as I became particularly critical of public education.

TWENTY

JOBLESS FOR THE SECOND TIME

I became certified to teach in the fall of 2002. However, I only obtained a certificate in history, something that worried my mentor very much. He was honest with me about the fact that it was going to very hard to get a teaching job with only a history certificate. Every district wanted teachers with a social studies composite certificate, not just history. Moreover, I was not a coach; therefore, landing a full-time job as a history teacher became an impossible ordeal. Countless interviews during the spring and summer of 2003 in every school district and almost every private school in the Houston area led to nowhere. By then, my choices were few; I could become a manager at Kroger, use my engineering and architecture skills in the oil company where my brother and dad worked, or continue with graduate school, hoping that I would eventually work at the college level. I decided to continue with graduate school. I earned my master's in education in the spring of 2003.

In 2003, I decided that I would immerse myself in the Social Education program. I stopped looking for a full-time job in teaching. I wanted to finish my master's and get in the doctoral program. I would spend entire days in the Social Education lab writing and doing research. The presence of other graduate students greatly influenced me. In the fall of 2003, I officially entered the doctoral program.

In the doctoral program, things took a completely different turn. In the spring of 2004, I presented a paper in a conference for the first time in almost seven years. Things went really well. People would not stop asking me questions. I was even invited to a working dinner with the chair of the session. Inside of me, I could only think about what a difference this was from architecture, where everything that could go wrong, did. At that time, I no longer cared to find a full-time job in teaching. I was savoring the life of a graduate student and the experience of academia. On the contrary, I loved the lazy and relaxed atmosphere of college more than the daily hectic grind of public schools, which I was very familiar with because of my years of substituting. I was actually very happy with substituting only once or twice a week and working at the store on the weekends. The university literally became my home from dawn to dusk during 2003.

Things, however, have their own twist of fate. From the beginning, Neil and Dr. White insisted that I should write about the disabled, and at first, I did not pay much attention to their suggestion. Influenced by Peter McLaren's (2003b) *Life in School* and *Cries from the Corridor*, all I wanted was to write about the corporate assault on education. Without sending a single résumé, or filling a single job application, the phone started to ring. Schools, where my résumé was kept on file, started to contact me again for an interview. One more time, I was getting interviews on a weekly basis. It is ironic how eventually I would end up working as a special education teacher.

In the summer of 2004, one of those schools in Houston's inner city contacted me. I was offered a summer job as a college tutor; I accepted the job. The job consisted of teaching summer school, along with a regular teacher as a supervisor, to the students who failed the state's mandated test known as TAKS (Texas Assessment of Knowledge and Skills). We needed to prepare them for the August TAKS retake. At that time, I met my teacher and mentor, Mrs. Ramos (not her real name), who was a veteran teacher with over thirty years of experience. From the beginning, she was very concerned that I was not teaching full-time. I told her one afternoon, over happy hour, my entire story. She decided to do something about it.

She talked to the principal, Mr. Campos. They did not have any job openings at the time. Under their recommendations, however, they decided to make me a full-time substitute teacher, until a full-time teaching opportunity became available. Mr. Campos knew me very well. He interviewed me early that spring for a paraprofessional opening. Nevertheless, under the advice of Mrs. Ramos, I never became a paraprofessional. According to her, doctoral students do not work as paraprofessionals. However, I never became a substitute teacher in Houston ISD. A week before school started in the fall of 2004, and the day before I was supposed to attend the new-employee training session for Houston ISD, the associate principal of the high school where I had substitute taught for so long called me. She offered me a job in special education, and I took it.

Destiny

If there is something that I will always remember from my grandmother, it is the fact that she always said that I should believe in destiny. The job that Mrs. Williams (not her real name) offered me was not in social studies but in special education. In the beginning, she offered me a resource math class and a resource social studies class. I wanted to teach regular history; however, I accepted the job with certain reservations.

In the beginning, I only taught for a half day. I was out by 10:30 in the morning, and this gave me the freedom to take afternoon and night classes at the university. In the spring of 2005, I became a full-time teacher. In addition to teaching resource math and social studies, I was teaching ESL. That spring, I became certified to teach special education and reading in ESL.

I did not make much of my first semester of teaching. Despite my critical view of education, I kept my views to my academic work at the graduate courses. I was just a regular teacher in the classroom. My youthful appearance and my college attitude assured me a good rapport with my students. Nothing out of the ordinary happened. My mind was at my graduate work and not at my work. Things, however, were going to change. As the semester progressed, I became tired. Discipline issues and the demand of the job started to weigh on me. I would leave my job as soon as I could and head for the university library, which became my refuge, where I would spend the rest of the evening decompressing.

Frustrated, on the verge of tears, I remember walking into the Social Education lab, where I ran into Neil, a colleague of mine. I had only been teaching for two months, and I was already emotionally exhausted. Also, by then, I was having a mental block about what to do and write in the doctoral program. Discipline issues, bureaucracy, night classes, and weekends in the library researching were taking a toll on me. I was not getting anything out of reading critical pedagogy. On the contrary, I was starting to become very cynical about it. A series of improper posts in my graduate cohort's blog, which made several of my friends and Dr. White upset, alerted me that something was not going right. Once again, the same dreadful feeling that I experienced in architecture was coming back. I told Neil that I did not want a repeat of what happened in architecture.

That afternoon, Neil grabbed a book called *The Moral and Spiritual Crisis in Education* by David Purpel (1989). He suggested it to me. I took the book, which belonged to Dr. White, but I did not read it. I just simply put the book on my desk and let it sit there until the Christmas Holidays. For some reason, that was the only book I took with me to Denver, during the holiday break of 2004. By then, I was desperate to get out of Houston.

It was in Denver that I read Purpel's book. For quite some time, since I started to visit Denver, I enjoyed going to a certain Starbucks to read or write. I guess the mountain scenery inspired me to read or write at that particular coffee shop. One afternoon, while my family went out holiday shopping, I requested them to leave me at that particular Starbucks. I needed to do some doctoral work. Purpel's book took me by storm, literally. I finished the book in one day. For the first time, I saw our failure to rethink education morally. This explained so much of what I was experiencing in the school. The great faith of our country in education was not equating with the proper response to educational needs by our society. In the end, this book opened my eyes.

When I got back from Denver, I was invigorated. I continued teaching, writing, and reading. However, I was not sure what to do, wanting only to write about what I saw—education, as an entity, unable to provide a meaningful experience to the average student. In the spring of 2005, I decided to go to Montreal for an educational conference for an entire week. It was there that everything took a turn in my doctoral career. Attending sessions about education and social justice, meeting people from all over the world, and exchanging ideas with students from the local universities greatly influenced me. I was walking one afternoon with Jason, a doctoral colleague, when he plainly told me that I needed to start writing about myself. He said that I had a story to tell. My experience as a Social Education student and a disabled teacher was unique. It was right there, in Montreal, that I decided to write a dissertation about myself.

TWENTY-ONE

FULL-TIME TEACHING

It is five in the morning, and the alarm sounds; I wake up and get out of bed. The day before, I stayed until ten thirty P.M. in my school, getting my classroom ready for the first day of classes. A custodian reminded me that in an hour the building was going to be closed. It is my first day as a teacher. Nervousness sinks in. As I drive to school, I can only think about how everything will play itself out. There is a funny sensation in my stomach. The only thought that ran through my mind is that I am a full-time teacher. Whether I was ready or not, that day was finally here.

The first week went fine. I got to meet my students. We started slow. After all, it was a resource class. By the second week, things started to take the normal route of a new and inexperienced teacher. I would send students to the office over minor discipline issues, as the administrator saw it. Unsure of what to teach in math, since it was a resource class, I would make last minute decisions on the spot. Over the course of the year, things got progressively worse, due to my lack of organization and discipline.

I finished my first year of teaching with mixed results. I did great in social studies. With one exception, my students passed the state-mandated test in social studies. I did miserably in ESL. The rest of the teachers on my team complained that I was not following the curriculum. Infighting emerged between the teachers and me. In the end, I told them that I would not accept an ESL position for the second year. Math was not my strong subject. I was not a math teacher. For the next year, Mrs. Williams decided that I would teach history, which is what I do to this day.

During my second year as a teacher, I was assigned to be a co-teacher with the World History team. With a reputation of having previous co-teachers who barely taught or knew the subject, the pressure was put on me to actually teach and help the team. My co-teacher, Coach Larry Emerson (not his real name), decided that I would take control of the later periods of the day, and he would teach the first two periods. I had known Larry for a long time. As a student teacher, I observed him. I also substituted for him on several occasions. In the end, we taught together for five years. In the classroom, things with Larry went very well. Co-teaching has allowed me to give the students the individual attention they need.

During my second year, I became a tracking teacher. In my school district, we are called case managers. Case managers are assigned to academically track a student throughout the year. We are liaisons between teachers and parents. We make sure the teachers are following the students' IEP (Individual Education Plan) and provide their accommodations. Being a case manger has opened my eyes in the last few years, greatly influencing my view of special education.

One day, I was sitting in an ARD (Admission, Review, and Dismissal) meeting. After much argument from a parent, a student, whom I tracked, was being released from special education services. The regular education teacher said, with an ironic tone, that now the student had become his problem. Students as problems? The student needed help. He was failing classes. However, the insistence from the parent that he did not need special services, along with certain bureaucratic maneuvering, prompted the administration to release the student.

Except for reading the IEPs (Individualized Education Plan) and presenting them to the committee, I sat quietly. However, I could not stop wondering about the fact that a teacher saw a student as a problem. Where did this mentality and frame of thinking come from? I wonder how many times I was a problem to my teachers. During this summer, I had a chance to attend an advanced placement workshop at Rice University to teach European History. The instructor, Ms. Heller, a veteran teacher from Oklahoma, asked the class whose responsibility it is to teach a student to properly write an essay. We said it was the English teacher's. She said it is ours as well; otherwise, she wondered why we decided to become teachers. For Ms. Heller, a history teacher is just as responsible for making sure a student knows how to properly write and do math.

We may disagree to what level an English teacher is responsible for a student doing well in math. However, my personal opinion is that we all are equally responsible. I want to take Ms. Heller's comment to a deeper level and believe that we, as teachers, got into teaching because we wanted to make a difference in someone's life. In the end, I want to believe that it is everyone's responsibility to make a student successful.

My experience, as a tracking teacher, is what shaped my current view of special education. It is a world filled with jargon and psychometrics that nobody seems to understand. If a student makes the mark and passes the test, then he or she is succeeding. In the meantime, the field becomes a place that teachers, students, and parents learn to hate. Students hate it because they are trapped. Teachers hate it because they are tired of the bureaucracy and demand, and parents hate it because the system is not working. The result is that we all give up, and we pound the doors, by the end of the year, wishing to get out and get a summer break.

One day, my best friend, John, told me that one of his students said that I was her favorite teacher. The reason is that I always gave her the answers. John said that was not good. However, with that student, I had developed a good rapport. She struggled through my class. I knew that if I expected her to do the drill and perform, she would not be successful. I could always simplify the assignment to where it was easy for her. Larry and I decided that the most important thing for her was to understand the subject. Moments like this make me wonder what is the real role of a teacher. It is my role to pass or fail a student. We do not pass or fail in life. We struggle, fail, make mistakes, hit rock bottom, get up, learn our lessons, and keep on going.

After my second year of teaching, my mind was set. I would write about special education and social justice. For one, I saw the field not working. I kept on wondering why teachers in my field were so angry and why students were not happy. I came to the conclusion that we, as a society, still are not sure what to make of education, deciding to put education on autopilot and let things happen. In the meantime, like Ron Miller (1990/1997) said, schools are becoming our worst social engineering project. The second reason is what we want special education to be. I was in a meeting when we were told that every special education student was going to be assessed by TAKS. If this is our measure of success or failure for a student receiving special services, we are in big trouble. As I reflect on my early years, it was not what I passed or failed in my classes that made me successful, but it was what I took from my experiences that made me who I am today. If we looked at my high school transcript, by conventional standards, I was doomed to failure.

My life as a disabled person is a life of struggles, proving people wrong when they tell me I cannot. It is also a life of pursuing my dreams. Right now, I am a teacher, a disabled teacher. Contrary to other teachers, I have been in my students' shoes myself. I sat in ARD meetings where I was told I could not go to college and be realistic about my life. I was told not to take certain classes because I was not going to be successful. Do I bring to my practice a special touch that other teachers do not have? I do not think so. I can point out scores of teachers in my school who I believe are far better at what they do than I am. Being a disabled teacher has brought something else to me. The system was not working for me, and I was not happy. As I see the same unhappiness one more time in my students, I wonder what school should be. I was not necessarily interested, as a student, in passing classes or making grades. I wanted somebody to listen to me, let me be the person that I wanted to be, and help me be the future architect that I wanted to be.

Being disabled is not easy. I can always see the face of students during the first day of school, as they watch me talk. However, as the year progresses, they learn to trust me. Do I wish I could speak, walk, and write better? Yes. However, it is not my concern to be more "normal." My disability is a fact of life, and it will stay with me to the very day I die. As a disabled teacher, it is not my disability for disability's sake that consumes my thoughts, but it is the fact that I am reliving in my students what I had to experience as a high school student myself.

As a disabled individual, I could easily be an example of success. I would rather not be that. I would prefer to see my position as one that my students could better. My struggles and my experiences are not unique, as I come to the realization that there are other people who may be in a better position to understand my struggles and where I come from. All I can say, as a disabled, is that my experiences are lived experiences, which allows me to help my students and their families to navigate a disempowering system. My disability is not about where I have been or where I am going, but about being able to look my students straight in their eyes and tell them directly how things are. It goes without saying that I often relate well to my students, which helps me to give them hope—the hope that all of us can actualize for all special education students.

It was on my way back to Houston from Montreal this last summer that I happened to sit next to a principal from a private school. She wondered why I became a teacher, if I went to college to be an architect. Not in the mood to tell her my life story, I told her I do not have an answer. "Things just happened," I said. We were silent during the remainder of the flight. The truth is that I still do not have an answer, and I still do not know why I became a teacher. Whatever answer I may have about making a difference in someone else's life, rings empty to me. I guess that by now, I have deeper reasons that explain why I became a teacher.

According to Purpel (Purpel & McLaurin, 2004), these are the best and worst of times for education. These are the worst of times because of what education has become, and these are the best of times because there has never been a more promising time to really change education. I want to believe that, as a teacher, these are my own best of times, where a better education experience can be envisioned for millions of disabled. My contributions as a disabled teacher will be minimal in the grand scheme of things. My hope, however, is that we make it better, as we struggle together.

TWENTY-TWO

THE MORAL AND SPIRITUAL REFLECTION

I must stress that my reflection is not limited only to special education, but to education in general. This is due to my firm belief that special education is not an isolated entity from the rest of public education, as many in the academic world have emphasized (Erevelles, 2002; Gabel, 2002; Hehir, 2005). It is, rather, an institution intimately connected to the rest of education, where, if anything, the problems and social confusions of education are accentuated to an even greater scale (Valentine, 2007).

After teaching for four years and attending a doctoral program with an emphasis in social justice, I based this project on my self-reflection by laying the foundation for investigating social justice issues in special education. In a sense, I describe my professional knowledge landscape (Clandinin & Connelly, 1995) and map my personal terrain of teaching (Hamilton, 1996).

I communicate my findings through journals, paper reflections, and conference presentations, and ad hoc means (e.g., private conversations, peer-to-peer conferences, and emails). These findings are the basis for my own self-dialectical and reflective process, which is the foundation of my empirical scholarship. Although it was not until the summer of 2006 that I decided to fully explore narrative inquiry as my methodology, questions and dialogues, as a self-dialectical process, started to arise much earlier. During my first days of in-service as a new teacher, I wrote in my journal:

> We started the year with a week of professional development in-service before school starts next week. I find it weird that one session after another is about what to do in order to not get sued. We have not had one single session dealing with how to empower, engage, or stimulate the special education student. We have not had a single session on how to improve reading, or writing, which is what I was

> looking for. I wonder why. This is the beginning of my career as a special ed teacher. I am already starting to have questions and doubts about this. Are we special ed teachers and educators? Or, are we legal servants who keep the district from getting sued?
>
> (Diary entry, August 4, 2004)

In the fall of 2005, I took my first of a series of classes by Dr. Cheryl Craig. I had to take several classes on research and methodology. As before, I did not know what to expect. Suddenly, I was introduced to the scholarship of Aoki (1989/1990), Bruner (1990), Schwab (1960, 1971) , Schön (1991), and Eisner (2006) to name a few. Over the last couple of years, one of the scholars who have greatly influenced me is Jerome Bruner. In his book, *Acts of Meaning*, Bruner (1990) talks about human psychology as a transaction of constructing meaning. For Bruner (1990), the conviction of reconstructing meaning is based upon two arguments. The first is that to understand a person you must understand his or her "intentional state," and "the second is that the form of this intentional states is realized only through participation in the symbolic system of culture" (Bruner, 1990, p. 33). This concept, when proposed by Bruner, radically changed the way we could see human experience, deviating from the previous form of biological experience, which does not cover the nature of our actions. Culture becomes a symbolic system—it entitles a system of language, modes, forms of discussion, and communal experience. This is what Bruner (1990) calls "cultural" or "folk psychology" (p. 35). People have used cultural or folk psychology to organize, explain, and understand social experiences. This is achieved through narrative, and in my case it is self-narrative (Ellis, 1997; Seaman, 2006):

> Today, Jason and I walked all over Montreal. We visited McGill and funky-town. He is not the first person who tells me to start writing about myself, and he is not the first person who tells me that I have a story to tell. However, what is my story? What do I write? What is it that I have to tell? Another disability story; I don't feel like it.
>
> (Diary entry, Montreal, April 2005).

By nature, humans are "story-telling animals" (Craig, 2006b, p. 263). We like to reconstruct visions of ourselves, so we can explore our identities and what shapes our lives. As Bruner (1996) argues, narrative is used as a mode to put our thoughts together. For me, this did not happen until the Christmas break of 1994. Never before in my life had I written or used a journal to keep my thoughts. After spending an entire afternoon in a Starbucks in Denver reading Purpel's (1989) *The Moral and Spiritual Crisis in Education*, thoughts started to flow, which I needed to put on paper:

> I never started a journal, or never put my thoughts on paper. I am not the kind of person who puts his feelings and thoughts on a piece of paper. I always wanted to do it, and I admire those who are able to do so. Nevertheless, previous attempts have failed. As I sit in this coffee shop, what is it that I want to write? On one hand, it is so uncomfortable to write about myself. I am simply not the kind of person who writes about his own life. However, I do feel the urge to write, and education is what I want to write about. Trivialized education? What does that mean? Evasion or neglect of larger, more critical topics in education? What does it mean to me? As I see my practice, I see a teacher, like the rest, surviving and merely keeping my head above water. When I wanted to become a teacher, I had a vision that school was going to be fun. The daily demands of paperwork, grading, meetings, and agendas are quickly erasing that. For some strange reason, this is beginning to look more like Kroger. I don't feel like a teacher—whatever that was supposed to feel like. I feel like a manager, like I felt at Kroger.
>
> (Diary entry, Denver, December, 2004)

After the Christmas break of 2004 in Denver and my trip to Montreal in the spring of 2005, my urge to write about education started. Influenced by critical pedagogy (Kincheloe, 2004; McLaren, 2003b), I started to question the basic economic, political, social, and cultural models of this nation. Questions about our nation's economic trend started when I was in architecture school. At that time, I saw that urban renewal did not translate into better housing and living conditions for the poor, but it was the creation of exclusive places where the rich could live their trendy lifestyles (Anyon, 2005). I think this an issue more poignant and urgent than ever before. As I wrote in my journal:

> This nation has an incredible amount of wealth, but it has also disenfranchised entire sectors of society. The best of healthcare is only available to those with deep pockets who are also able to afford the best education, the best housing and the best prospects in life. To be disenfranchised in this nation is very serious. The poor and unemployed in this nation must face a terrible predicament. This predicament means lack of welfare assistance, unemployment benefits, subsidized childcare and affordable healthcare. Furthermore, the urban poor may face further displacement and dislocation. Inner city renovation, urban renewal, or downtown revival has not translated into better urban schools, employment opportunities for the urban poor, or the mass scale renovation of inner city neighborhoods. Inner city renovation or urban renewal has meant the building of high-end entertainment centers, overpriced apartments, and fashionable coffee shops.
>
> (Undated diary entry, 2005).

My views about education became greatly influenced by my view of the corporate encroachment of capitalistic ideals (McLaren & Farahmandpur, 2005; Talbert, 2002). In the new age of education, we do find little disagreement in the fact that the public schools have been preoccupied with educating democratic citizens. Nevertheless, the fact that the main purpose of schools has been to produce a ready-to-work labor force for the economy has become undeniable (Kincheloe, 2007; Singh, Kenway, & Apple, 2005). It is in the Western public schools where, according to Kincheloe (2007), corporate interests have been consolidated. This is what Kincheloe (2007) refers to as "democratic economy" (p. 25). As my doctoral years progressed, this view started to take shape.

However, as the years went by, this quest for social justice in general education morphed unintentionally into the quest for social equality in special education and disability studies, which in great part was fueled by my own personal experience. Since the creation of the social model of disability studies in the UK (Mitra, 2006; Oliver, 1986; Reiser, 2006a), it has been accepted that the disabled also face social barriers, impeding their social, cultural, political, and economic fulfillment (Baglieri & Knopf, 2004; J. Shapiro, 1998). The result is the acknowledgement that disabled individuals are also oppressed (Apple, 2001; Ferri & Connor, 2005; Gabel, 2002; Ho, 2004). Throughout my life, this has been pretty much my experience and my feeling. As I wrote:

> One day, during my sophomore year in high school, I was devastated. Earlier in the day, I argued with my counselor and the special education diagnostician for an hour and half. I learned that my grade point average (GPA) was lower because I was in special education. My GPA would always be less than the GPA on the regular education track. I would never make it to the top ten like my brother, who was not disabled. It did not matter how good my grades were, how many A's I made, and how hard I tried. I made it clear to them that I did not want to be in Special Education anymore.
>
> (Excerpt from my candidacy paper, spring 2007)

On the other hand and since the publication of Freire's (1970) Pedagogy of the Oppressed, it has been contested that much needs to be done to end inequality in education (Anyon, 2005; Kincheloe, 2004; McLaren, 2003b; McLaren & Farahmandpur, 2005). It is undeniable that, since the enactment of PL 94–142 and IDEA (Individuals with Disabilities Education Act), the disabled community has achieved an incredible amount of public recognition and legal protection against discrimination (Osgood, 2005). However, influenced by critical pedagogy and moral education, I started to have questions of a moral nature in the field of disability studies:

> I still remember how tired I was in Denver. How much I wanted to quit my job and grad school. Thank God I opened Purpel's book in Denver last year. The questions that I had about regular ed, I now have for special ed. It makes so much sense now. I see the same evasion of issue in general ed also happening in special ed. I wonder if the same questions regarding general ed in terms of grading, political and social evasion, and the cultural trivialization of education are also part of special ed. Is anybody asking these questions? Is anybody asking how oppressive special ed is? After reading Purpel, it seems to me that we have not paused for a moment

> and wondered what kind of learning environment we want for our disabled students. I don't see that happening in special ed.
>
> (Diary entry, April 2006, San Francisco)

Later I wrote:

> Today, I sat in another ARD meeting. Another ARD where a student is told to be realistic about college and a degree. Another ARD where a student is told that he will never make it. What would have happened if I listened to those who told me to be realistic about architecture, college, and a degree? Have we learned something in the last few years? I think we have not.
>
> (Diary entry, Houston, May 2006)

Along the way, the process led me to a paradigm shift: that any "set of problems" (however defined or localized) that emerged from special education cannot be solved by the imposition of rigid structures and mechanisms. Forcing a solution to a problem would create another problem, and a defined set of pedagogical guidelines cannot be imposed. As such, only the human experience would be developed. As I wrote in an entry in my tentative research proposal paper:

> It is not my goal to write "how to go about" liberating students as a role of the special education teacher, despite my temptation to do so. My biggest hope is to clarify our need to do it. I do not pretend to provide a version of liberating pedagogy for the disabled more than the need to do so. My biggest goal is to propose why we desperately need to do so.

I came to see the full dimension of this experience as those "things" (such as the spiritual, theoretical, moral, and affectionate) currently silenced by the standard-based model of education (White, et al., 2007):

> As a social educator and a doctoral student, there are several questions I wish I could ask. However, at this moment, the question that I really want to ask is why social education? What kind of citizens do we want to produce? This is the most impending question right now. Are we producing automatons for the working place and the corporate world or active and participating citizens? How do we

> define such participations? With that participation, what do we want to accomplish? Social education for me, therefore, will mean the awareness of evasion of critical and important issues. What are the real crises facing this nations? How may such crises affect education? How do I ask this and other questions regarding social education? Rather than merely asking and answering the questions, I propose narrative. With the narrative, the question becomes personal, integrated, and it will have depth. Social education functions best with me when it is a personal endeavor. It is when I search my innermost emotions, passions and intrigues that social education becomes a colorful kaleidoscope of endless possibilities. Why social education? Why not psychology, engineering, medicine or anything else? Because social education for me is awareness. It is an awareness of the social reality of this nation and how this reality has its roots in the current educational sphere.
>
> (Undated diary entry, sometime in the summer of 2006).

In that framework, I moved away from addressing issues in special education (moving away from formal qualitative and quantitative research) to understanding approaches that take into account the wider human experience (moving beyond research and dialogue). In this regard, books such as *What Is School For?* (R. Miller, 1990/1997) and *The Moral and Spiritual Crisis in Education* (Purpel, 1989) were used as anchoring sets of literature. As I wrote in the summer of 2006:

> Miller (1990/1997) wonders if we are seriously considering a better educational environment. I wonder if that is the case for special education. And if it is, what shape would that have? What is it that we are truly looking for?
>
> (Diary entry, summer 2006)

The moral accounts, underlying the premises of education, provided me an entryway to formulate my own action research. Purpel's *The Moral and Spiritual Crisis in Education* (1989) provided the immediate contextualization of the argument. Purpel (1989) argues that education has been trivialized, referring to two major phenomena in the educational discourse. The first is the "evasion or neglect of larger, more critical topics" (Purpel, 1989, p. 19). The second is "the stress put on technical rather than on social, political, and moral issues" (Purpel, 1989, p. 19). The stress on the technical is our emphasis on testing, merit pay, and teaching efficacy:

> So, this is what these so called content days in October are. TAKS, TAKS, and more TAKS. How do we improve the scores? How can we engage the students more. . . . .so they can pass TAKS? Every minute is supposed to be instructional time. Do these people realize what schools are becoming?
>
> (Diary entry, October 10, 2005)

In his argument, Purpel (1989) asserts that responses to the educational crises have been "at best ameliorative" rather than showing a deeper commitment to address the basic culture of our institutions (Purpel, 1989, p. 19), which for me meant that schools are impersonal. Again, in October of 2005 I wrote:

> Why are schools in Texas so impersonal? Teachers are just giving instruction. They are not willing to develop deeper relationships with students. When I was little, I was told school was my second home, and teachers were my second set of parents. I wonder if that is a concept taught in the US.
>
> (Diary entry, October 15, 2005)

Once the frame was set, I pushed forward the action and dialogue of the research. From the moral argument about general education, arguments about special education of a moral nature emerged:

> It is very unlikely that the current moral crisis and spiritual turmoil of American education would miss the disability and special education field. It would also be very improbable that the mountainous attacks from a disgruntled public, in the form of angry parents, homeschooling advocates, free-market advocates, magnet school proponents, private school vouchers supporters, and religious groups do not affect the field providing services to children in special needs
>
> It would be hard to believe that the special education teacher could remain immune to the current craze promoting standardized

testing, curriculum assessment, multicultural studies, inclusion, portfolio requirements, ecological classrooms, Afro-centric and Latino-centric curricula, and an infinite sea of other concerns bombarding the rest of the profession.

The sad reality is that the field of special educationhas not escaped these attacks. On the contrary, the disability field is the battlefield for inclusionists, tracking advocates and dissenters, social model proponents, medical model defenders, and radical visionaries as a modern version of a colonial war map. Parents have amassed a legion of legal protectors and advocates. Teacher are inundated by the demand to legally implement individual educational plans (IEP), modified curriculum, documentations, ARD (admission, dismissal, and review) committees' demands, and the list goes on.

(Semester paper, spring of 2007)

De-contextualization

The pressure of the modern educational system (political, bureaucratic, standardized, systemic, cultural) does not allow the teacher to de-contextualize the curriculum of knowledge (White, et al., 2007). Instead, such an environment only allows for insular, fragmented, and detached learning, discouraging the presence of human experience (see Polanyi, 1966). What is encouraged is the isolated learning events, which never takes into consideration the larger cultural context of the environment. This also discourages learning from personal experiences, allowing only room for tacit knowledge (Polanyi, 1966). I will refer to tacit knowledge as an unspoken form of knowledge where things are suggested only through silence. Polanyi (1966) refers to tacit knowing as the visual interpretation characterized by scientific inquiry:

> We may say that a scientific discovery reduces our focal awareness of observations into a subsidiary awareness of them, by shifting our attention from them to their theoretical coherence (p. 3).

As Polanyi (1966) warns us, scientific observation might have the danger of being distant, which only allows for a marginal observation from the point of origin. However, how can we understand tacit knowing? Let me point to an example. Since I was very young, I have been an avid swimmer. I learned to swim before I learned to walk. I started to walk at the age of three. For years, I used swimming for muscular therapy. I know how to swim, and I can provide swimming lessons; however, I cannot fully describe the muscular actions that allow me to swim. In the same light, Polanyi (1966) has described tacit knowing as the exercise so evident in education where students learn to label, describe, and classify. Nevertheless, the exact knowledge of understanding how something happened is not taught. The best way to put this into context is an example that happened to me during a geology class I took for fun in college. We labeled and classified rocks and minerals, but we never learned how to understand the nature of a rock or a mineral. We know that even in the most rigorous types of scientific process, the human experience prevails (Ellis, 1997; Polanyi, 1961).

By moving away from tacit knowledge, we can start to use de-contextualization, allowing us to separate ourselves from the official knowledge embedded in the field of education. In other words, I started to question things and not take them for granted. As Conle (1999) describes, the teacher is submerged in the technocratic nature of the practice, which never takes into consideration the human experiences of the environment. In the case of special education, tacit knowledge has produced dire consequences. It has become an agency which for the most part is submerged in the technocratic nature of education. Special education, so far, has involved the interpretation of data (Hehir, 2005; S. R. Miller, 1981; Valentine, 2007). Nevertheless, the constant thirst for data has deviated the practitioner from looking at the education of the disabled from a broader social, economical, and cultural context (Mariage, Paxton-Buursma, & Bouck, 2004; Valentine, 2007). Valentine (2007) argues that little exists in terms of looking at the human nature of special education. This became evident to me when I started to track special education students, during my second year of teaching:

> Is this how all ARD meetings are, where the only things that matter are numbers, scores, and assessments? Does anybody care how he felt? Does anyone care about his feelings about school? Everyone sat in the meeting wondering why he misbehaved. What about if school

> is no longer working for him? What about if the system, as we know it and as it is designed, no longer works for him?
>
> (Diary entry, fall of 2005)

As my practice in special education evolved, it became evident to me that the tacit nature of special education involves a culture of silence. This is a tacit nature that, according to Valentine (2007), has created a deafening void on more critical issues. According to Mariage, Paxton-Buursma, and Bouck (2004), this is very much true when we consider that the field of education is not a place where a diverse set of voices are listened to, outside of those voices of authority. This became very true for me:

> Another ARD, and this is another ARD where my voice does not count. My only role is to present the PLOP (present level of performance) and the IEP (individualized education plan) goals. I am starting to think that my role as a tracking teacher is purely clerical. At no time, was I asked how he is doing in my class, what we discuss on a daily basis, or how we relate to each other.
>
> (Diary entry, spring of 2006)

The tacit nature of special education leads me to two conclusions. The first is that it has become more comfortable to rely on the medical model, which implies that disability is a condition embedded in the individual, needing to be corrected from within (Burchardt, 2004; Handley, 2003). Within the medical disability model, the dominant perception is that limitations experienced by the disabled can be empirically explained by the individual's physical or mental conditions (Handley, 2003; Longmore, 1995). Like in the rest of the educational field, this tacit nature fits well the purpose of those in charge. Bound by legal ramifications, it would appear that it is far easier to focus on the narrow perspective of data, measurement, psychometrics, and numerical scales. We find it hard to dwell in the complex task of asking what is seriously working in special education.

The second conclusion of the tacit nature of special education leads me to believe that we, as a society, are simply afraid to ask complex moral questions regarding the field (Purpel, 1989). This might be due in part to the manic and schizophrenic nature of the profession (Valentine, 2007), which drives the average special education teacher to mere modes of survival:

> I am tired. Exhausted. All I want to do is chill, and sit in the lounge at UH this afternoon. I simply want to do nothing. I am tired of running around all morning filling papers, doing surveys, finishing ARD work, and so on. This is definitely not what I pictured special education to be. I never imagined this from special education. Thank God there is UH. Thank God there is a place where I can relax, get a coffee, read, and write. Otherwise, I would be literally punching holes in the wall.
>
> (Diary entry, spring of 2006)

However, I believe that the most uncomfortable reason why we are not asking more complex moral question is our inability to envision a different kind of education for our students. A form of education where the teacher is not a mere dispenser of authoritative knowledge (Freire, 1970; McLaren, 2003b), but rather a form of education in which teachers and students create empowering spaces where everyone collaborates together (Kincheloe, 2004). Sadly, the technocratic nature of education (Conle, 1999), which drowns teachers and administrators in mere modes of survival, does not allow those involved in the field time to reflect and envision a better form of education. There might be an array of reasons for this: job security, accountability, compliance, curriculum demands, and so on. The results are the same, a field fraught with uncertainties on how to make students successful and how to achieve it.

Moral and holistic education act as the catapult for the deconstruction of situational knowledge and this tacit nature, encouraging a rigorous context of meaningful reflection and dialogue about the missing dimension of experience, particularly in light of the hard questions asked in *The Moral and Spiritual Crisis in Education* (Purpel, 1989).

> On the one hand, there is very little disagreement in what we want our schools to be. Schools are the places, as Purpel wrote (1989), where we expect our students to become citizens, social models, and where they learn to read, write, and do math. Schools are the places where parents send their children to be productive members of

> society. However, we drill instruction endlessly. Students are expected to attend the same schedule day after day. Does anyone ever question this? Where do these appalling sets of standards come from? What would happen if students had a more flexible college schedule? What would happen if school ended at noon? What would happen if teachers could only teach for 20 hours a week and have the rest of time to prepare their lessons? What would happen if we were allowed to have end-of-the-year parties? What would happen if schools were more humane?
>
> (Reflection, undated)

This helped me reflect on my own school experience as a special education teacher, student, and individual. *The Moral and Spiritual Crisis in Education* (1989) became crucial for me, allowing for the formulation of the classroom we ought to have. As I later reflected:

> Last year, there was not an afternoon in which I did not come to UH frustrated and tired. It was hard for me to understand why. Schools are prisons. They are prisons not only for students, but for teachers as well. The bell-to-bell schedule, the rules, and the demands apply to teachers as well.
>
> (Reflection, Spring 2007)

In my research, the process of de-contextualizing the educational setting has greatly helped me. It has allowed me to detach myself from the insular knowledge embedded in the teaching experience, which is an experience that does not allow the teacher to decipher and understand the environment in which he or she finds himself or herself. This is an experience which, so far, only allows the average teacher to conform to the rigid structure of society's rules for education. Purpel (1989) argues that one of the biggest failures of the educational reforms in this nation is the lack of reconceptualization of the schooling process, which for the most part I also see happening in special education:

> I agree with Purpel (1989). Much of the civil rights movements were not truly radical. They were movements designed to improve existing living conditions within the pre-set structural social settings. Could this be also true for special education? I am afraid that the disability

> movement did not challenge core cultural beliefs towards the disabled. It simply ameliorated our existence within the same rigid social structures. How otherwise can we explain the special education setting?
>
> (Undated diary entry, sometime in 2007)

As Purpel (1989) argues, many of the educational reforms have been to simply make things better within the existing framework. Such insight has helped me question more rigorously the special education setting as whole. It has helped me, in the end, envision a more critical approach to special education:

> If I tell my colleagues that today we dismantled all the calculators that I brought to my students in the resource math class, they would be appalled. However, I am appalled at what I saw. Did these students ever dismantle anything? Did they ever get the urge to pull anything apart and see what it looked like inside? Are they curious to do anything like this at all? I imagined that if there was a place where we could do stuff like this, it would be in the resource classes. But no, we are supposed to drill, drill, and drill. And when we can't drill anymore, we are supposed to get strength from who knows where and drill some more. I have only taught special ed for a little while, and I can only see what a boring place this is to teach.
>
> (Diary entry, spring of 2005)

Later I wrote:

> OK, if there is a place where I expect to see people become more critical of the special education process, it is at AERA (American Education Research Association). To sit in a session where numbers, data, and statistics were shown to provide information about how to help a disabled student pass state-mandated tests is just sickening to me. This is not what I expected to see here.
>
> (Diary entry, San Francisco, 2006)

Responsiveness and Questioning

As I began to de-construct the field of special education, I began to be responsive and reflective about education. The task was not easy;

however, it invited me to creative and reflective spaces where these fragmentized forms of experiences could be understood. At first I struggled:

> OK. First, what do I write about special education? My experience as a student, as a teacher, or as a grad student? What is it that I can say, which has never been said before? Do I simply conduct a survey? Do I simply interview other colleagues and their experiences?
>
> (Reflection, spring of 2006)

I began to rethink "special" education within a moral and holistic view, which allowed me to envision special education from a cultural context (Miller 1990/1997; Purpel, 1989). I started to ask questions about special education that I had never asked before:

> Did we really know what we were doing? Did PL 94–142 accomplish what it was supposed to do? Or, did we just simply dump the disabled students in the same denigrating classroom that the general population was dumped in?
>
> (Diary entry, spring of 2007)

As time passed, I could start to see the connection to critical pedagogy (Apple, 2001; Giroux, 1988, 2003a; Kincheloe, 2004) and moral education (Purpel, 2003; Purpel & McLaurin, 2004; H. S. Shapiro, 1998) to special education:

> As I sit here in San Francisco, listening to Mclaren and Kincheloe, I would imagine that nobody thinks about the marginalized and special education. We can talk about marginalization, the classroom, and social justice. I wonder how that can be envisioned for the disabled. Aren't disabled marginalized as well? As I see scores of my colleagues back in Houston distraught and frustrated by the profession, I can see special education in crisis as well.
>
> (Diary entry, San Francisco, spring of 2006)

I began to rethink "special" education within a moral and holistic education light, which allowed me to view special education from a cultural context (Miller 1990/1997; Purpel, 1989). As Purpel argue (1989, 2004), my reaction was to start seeing special education as trivialized. The trivialization of education is defined by Purpel (1989) as the neglect of larger social, political, economic, and cultural topics on education, which reduces the education discourse to topics of efficacy, merit pay, teacher performance, and student assessment. Like Miller (1990/1997), I began to see the field of special education in crisis. Miller (1990/1997) defines this crisis as the constant demand placed on the field without the inability to find a common path towards unity. Like in general education, I realized that we seldom tend to connect education to our most pressing social and cultural concerns of our time:

> I was asked to teach this resource social studies class. I was supposed to make them good citizens. The school definition of citizenship is that they know the importance of voting, getting a job, and in the case of special education, that students know that they can enroll in the armed forces. Does citizenship not involve knowing about what is going on in the world?
>
> (Diary entry, fall of 2005)

The engaging questions of holistic and moral education invited me to the opening of deeper forms of consciousness, which challenges the one-dimensionality of the technical nature of special education. This encouraged rigorous responses to the fragmentation of standard-based knowledge, which is sponsored by modern education (McNiff, 2007). I, acting as a teacher, began to form my own state-of-conscious development, leading to deeper understanding of the practice. However, such exercises also allowed for more rigorous questioning of the motives of the field as a whole, especially in the light of the new desire to test special education children with state-mandated tests:

> I cannot imagine what it is going to be like if all special ed students are going to take TAKS, even if it is modified. If this is our best response to measure the achievement of disabled students, we are in trouble. Is anybody thinking what the classroom will become for them? We are forced to be dispensers of knowledge, no longer educators.
>
> (Diary entry, spring of 2007)

In the end, by responding to the process of contextualization, I was able to move forward and have deeper reflections. Questions started to emerge that never surfaced before. What kind of classroom do we want for our special education students? What do we really want special education to be? Do we really care about the educational experiences of the special needs student? By using moral and holistic education as main pillars, empirical questioning started to emerge.

Holistic and moral education came to be understood as framework for empirical questioning. This encouraged me to wrestle with rigorous questions such as "What is special education for?" or "Who really benefits in special education?"

> I kept on wondering: How were my students in special education oppressed? How was I, as teacher and disabled, oppressed as well? What was it that made special education banking education? As a teacher, am I an oppressor also? It was not easy for me to make sense of these questions. In addition, to some extent, it continues to be a hard task for me to this day.
>
> (Excerpt from my candidacy paper, spring 2007)

This process helped me to formulate an interaction between critical, moral, and special education with my narrative. I made concrete what would not be evident (in the classroom and scholarship; in the dialogue between moral, holistic, and special education). It also guided me to acknowledge that in the search for something unknown, that "unknown" could be eluded in the act of searching (Matthiessen, 1978).

The exact definition of empirical is "observation derived by experience." I began to explore the educational landscape in which I found myself belonging. In the beginning, I must confess that finding the right path between critical pedagogy, moral education, social justice, and special education was not easy. Nevertheless, it allowed me to wrestle with very fundamental questions and dilemmas about my experience as a teacher:

> It feels good to me when they sit quiet and complete their work. It feels like a very productive day. However, I wonder. I wonder if this is the right way. I wonder if serious and good teaching is when they sit, stay quiet, and do what I ask them to do. I wonder what will happen if they start to question why they need to do this or that. I wonder what will be my reaction.

(Diary entry, fall of 2005)

Later I wrote:

> Am I an oppressor? On the one hand, I clamor for a liberating class. However, during the day, I see myself complying with my role as a teacher whose only expectations from above are to teach the curriculum.
>
> (Diary entry, spring of 2007)

Critical/Spiritual Transformation

Since the start, the nature of this project was to unravel the nature of the pedagogical process. I was not seeking a set of pedagogical ready-to-use set of ideas, but a foundation for a moral dialogue in special education. In order to keep this process as a live experience, I moved away from a systematic structure of reflection. This was done to keep the process open and fluid, which required a Socratic process of questioning, enabling the dislodging of pre-conceived notions of reality and self-knowing (Purpel, 1989). By doing this, I could question the very foundation of the fragmented and standardized form of education from the Neoliberal establishment (Hursh, 2006), which has also invaded the realms of special education (Apple, 2001).

Critically looking at special education has done two things for me. The first is to question the initial intent of the field. In my quest for answers, the moral foundation of special education is not mentioned or questioned. The general consensus is that special education was set in motion to give the disabled opportunities not available to them before (Blomgren, 1998; Hehir, 2005). I tend to agree. There was a time in history when to be a disabled meant being institutionalized and displaced (Burch & Sutherland, 2006; Covey, 1998; Stiker, 1999). Nevertheless, this does not stop me from questioning the current state of special education:

> I have faith that the example of liberation for one group (e.g., Freire's Brazilian peasants) can empower others to follow the example. It must also be remembered that the disabled have not been oppressed exclusively due to their impairment, but also in their racial, economical, and social entity. Pedagogical scholars, across the board,

> need to address the fact that, at times, disability is only one component of oppression in the life of an impaired person.
>
> (Excerpt from my first draft of candidacy paper, spring 2007)

One more time, I have to turn to Purpel (1989) and Valentine (2007). As I go to work everyday, I see a frantic scenario of special education teachers, struggling to survive and meet the daily demands that the system puts on them: meeting curriculum standards, doing paperwork, educating the students, and producing results. I believe that there is not a teacher in a classroom right now who at one point or another did not enter the profession with a genuine desire to teach and help students learn. Nevertheless, I do believe that the current teaching environment robs the teacher of that desire. We may have an array of answers to explain such a phenomenon. My personal take is that we have not engaged ourselves in questioning the basic standards of education and society. Critically thinking about education has helped me question those standards:

> The more I think of school, the more I think it is a prison: the bell-to-bell schedule, the rushed lunch, the discipline, the rules, the lack of windows and fresh air, and the constant demand to make the students follow the rules. Has anyone asked these kinds of questions before?
>
> (Diary entry, 2006)

It is true that originally I used this critical thinking to question the very foundation of general education (White, et al., 2007) to foster a more empowering classroom for the teacher and the student. Nevertheless, as the project morphed into a more critical view of special education, those critical questions turned into moral questions:

> Today, a teacher demanded that I put a modification sheet in her box about a student. Do we need to have a mods sheet to help a student? Do teachers no longer help a struggling student regardless of mods or not? What about if there were no ARD meetings? In Argentina and Venezuela, teachers simply helped me. It seemed that some things were done out of a common sense.
>
> (Diary entry, fall of 2006)

The responsibility of transformation falls to the individual, whether teacher, educator, professor, or outside observer. The inner-work of a spiritual transformation cannot be measured or quantified. The only thing that can be reported is an observer's version of a human event:

> I would probably have continued searching for a topic to research on social studies, perhaps started a survey or analyzed a distant topic of social justice in education, except that my life was turning upside down within me. In a matter of one year, my sister left the country to live in a foreign land, and one more time a Pohl member was going far, indeed very far away. Then, my brother, who was my lifetime partner in crime, got married; his new life as a married man and my life as single man did not coincide or have anything in common anymore. I became exhausted by the demand of my teaching profession, and I became very tired . . . very quickly of graduate school. This forced me to seek comfort and solace, not in education, but in evocative literature and in the therapy of writing.
>
> (Excerpt from my first methodology draft, fall 2007)

Although certain conditions and environments can be sought to construct the ideal conditions where this transformation exists, the imposition of guidelines of "progress" goes against the spirit of holistic or moral education and a vision of special education as a form of human experience for that matter. As White, Liss, and Marsh (2007) argue, holistic and moral education are not parcels of the pedagogical experience that we can teach, what can be reported is the participant's spiritual commitment of his or her transformation.

My spiritual transformation took place over my whole life. As a child, I cherished those precious moments when school was fun and an act of discovery. The tempera paint story, which I mentioned before, is not the only story I have in kindergarten. In kindergarten, there was a real locomotive in the yard. We played in that locomotive and learned how trains worked. I also broke the window of the life-size dollhouse. As a high school student, I wonder what would have happened if I listened to those who told me no. As a graduate student, I wonder what would have happened if I never entered education in the first place. I imagine my life would be different.

Thanks to education and my doctoral research, I have the chance to critically examine my life as a disabled person and a teacher. Disability has been part of my entire life; however, it was not until I became a doctoral student that I started to reflect what it meant for me to be disabled. As White, Liss, and Marsh (2007) argue, holistic and moral education are not parcels of the pedagogical experience that can we can teach. I cannot teach people what it means to be disabled. I can only transmit how it feels. However, every experience is unique. I am fully independent; nobody has to bathe me, wash me, feed me, or clothe me. In the end, I can only transmit my experience and the narrative of my life. Mark Seaman (2006) reminds us in his dissertation that experiences cannot be quantified. I imagine that experiences entail profound personal transformations, which shape our personality and the way we view the world. This is what happened to me as I began to reflect on my life and my educational experience. This project has helped me in this spiritual transformation.

TWENTY-THREE

FINAL REFLECTION

> Some teachers blamed the erosion on the effects of the economic downturn in the oil patch, which had dealt Odessa a crippling blow. Some blame it on the breakdown of the family unit; more and more kids were living with single parents who had to work morning, noon, and night just to make ends meet and didn't have the time or the inclination to promote the virtue of doing well in school. Some blame it on parents who seemed less interested in pushing their kids in the classroom than in football or band or choir. Some blame it on themselves, acknowledging that the passion they had for teaching twenty years ago had run dry. Some blame it on recent educational reforms passed in Texas that instead of making the classroom more stimulating, more creative, had the opposite by turning the teacher into a glorified clerk forced to follow an endless series of rules and procedures.
>
> H. G. Bissinger (2004, p. 132), *Friday Night Lights*

Twelve years have passed since my life took an unexpected turn. I never intended to become a teacher, much less a doctoral student in education and social justice. I never intended to confront my disability, be part of the special education field as a professional, and write a dissertation about what all these mean. My friend Mark Seaman (2006) said in his dissertation that presenting a narrative inquiry study is like driving a car without a map or directions: chances are you will end up in an unexpected place. This is because projects of this nature, according to Seaman (2008), constantly redefine themselves, perpetually evolving into new forms.

I consider this project a road trip without a map; I am constantly ending up in unexpected places. This is because I do not consider this project an isolated piece of work, but a continuation of a life experience, as a teacher, trained architect, immigrant, disabled, and social justice advocate. This road trip is not over, and I hope that it never ends.

Over the years, I have learned to cherish the experience of ending in unexpected places, letting me spiritually grow from arriving at such unplanned destinations. In this project, I explored my work in the a form of fluid inquiry (Joseph Schwab, 1960), which explores my personal and professional landscape (Clandinin & Connelly, 1995). Like many narrative inquiries preceding this one, the aim here is not to discover some truth or find the silver bullet, but to offer the narrative of my work and experience, arguing for the need of a moral and ethical discourse in special education.

My Experience

The narratives in this work are my life experiences, which include those moments of triumph, despair, success, and failure, along with the recognition that no experience is similar to another—each is unique in its own way. I refrained from looking at my experiences from the lens of what worked and what did not work, despite my initial temptation to do so. What became more important for me, as this project morphed and took this unexpected shape, was to ponder upon my experiences inside and outside the classroom. I make no claim to be a star teacher, nor do I claim to have solutions about how to teach special education students. On the contrary, I want my narrative to reflect the experiences of a teacher who is struggling and surviving through the labyrinth of public education and the system of special education. Moreover, if anything, I want my experiences to spark the desire of other teachers to learn and grow from their own experiences.

My experiences are many. As a teacher, working constantly in the trenches, I struggle with the daily grind of lesson planning, grading, meetings, parent conferences, and everything else that encapsulates the responsibility of being a teacher. Over the years, I must admit that I have grown to enjoy my job, and I work with an excellent team of colleagues, who have supported me professionally, emotionally, and personally in my doctoral endeavor.

However, my experiences in education are not limited to the classroom. I have been very fortunate to become a doctoral student. This was not an easy decision for me—as it was not an easy decision to become a teacher. However, I want to believe that this time, in this trip without a map or directions, I ended in a very happy place. This is a place where I have grown as a person and an individual, allowing me to explore the innermost corners of my soul for a true spiritual transformation. If it was not for such experience, I believe that my vision of education, society, and life would have been very narrow-minded. I may have become a teacher; however, I do not believe that I would have acquired the critical view of education that I have right now without my doctoral experience. I believe that this is the place that keeps me young, energetic, and enthusiastic about education.

As I said in the beginning, my experiences are many, and this project helped me to learn from such experiences. Through the art of writing, I have been able to uncover what I learned from such experiences, believing that the process of engaging in narratives is an experience in uncovering "the truth" in its own unique way (Ellis, 1997, p. 129).

The Critical in Me

I see teachers struggling everyday with the monumental demands of the profession. I cannot help but think that somewhere along the line this profession has the danger of draining the individual of his or her original desire and passion for teaching as a vocation or a calling; I want to believe that somewhere, deep in our souls, these were the reasons we joined the profession. However, I am afraid that, for many teachers, this profession puts them in survival mode—it forces the teacher into a mere daily struggle.

Several times, colleagues have told me to look at my profession solely as one that pays the bills. I have resisted this notion, trying hard to look at teaching as a life experience rather than a mere job. Perhaps my unique situation, as a disabled, has helped me to look at the profession differently. Critically, I find it detrimental that teaching can be reduced to something like this.

I still remember the comments of a doctoral colleague, Dr. Judy Owens, who said that nothing could affect the students more than their education—what they experience within the fours walls of a school, they will carry for the rest of their lives. Without a doubt, I will carry what I have experienced with my teachers, from kindergarten to graduate school, for the rest of my life. I want to believe that my students will carry forever what I do in the classroom; therefore, I resist looking at teaching as a job that pays the bills. This is not to say that I have not encountered teachers who are passionate and dedicated about their work. On the contrary, for every burned-out teacher that I have come across, I have encountered twice as many teachers who are profoundly committed, energetic, young-spirited, and enthusiastic about their profession. Perhaps it is their examples of dedication, professionalism, and devotion that encouraged me to become one of them.

Airport's Walkways

The state of teaching, as a profession, can emotionally drain a teacher, and it is not the only thing that I am critical about in regards to education. Like the rest of my social education cohort, I am critical of what happens in the classroom. Seaman (2008) uses the analogy of the long airport's mechanical walkways in that regard. He says that teaching is like walking forward in the wrong direction on an airport's walkway. You need to constantly move forward—if you stop moving forward, you will move backward. I truly believe that education is also placed on an airport's walkway. Some of us are struggling to move forward, while others have given up. As Seaman (2008) argues, when one stops walking against the wrong direction on the airport's walkway, one may tend to think that one has become stagnant. In reality, one is regressing.

It is ironic for me, as a critical pedagogue, to see how very little education has changed from the days that I was a student receiving the services. I see education regressing rather being stagnant. In the first decade of the new millennium, I find it very problematic that traditional teaching methods which are decades old continue to prevail. In the age of breathtaking technological advances, I find it ironic that the average classroom has not redefined itself accordingly;

the average classroom continues to be dominated by traditional lectures, transparencies, worksheets, notes, and homework. What is most scary to me, however, is to see how little debate situations like this generate.

One day, I visited an old friend in the architecture college at UH, who now teaches in the college's studios. He reminded me about how much I struggled making the models by hand, due to my disability. Today, students in architecture schools use laser-guided machineries to do their models, which cut the boards with microscopic precision. All drawings are drawn on computers—hand-drawn blueprints are no longer accepted.

I am not suggesting introducing laser-guided machinery in the public schools. Although I already know the answer from my friends in my doctoral cohort: Why not? However, I cannot help but wonder why public education has changed very little throughout the decades. My guess is that if public universities, which are known to be bastions of inflexible old traditions that are decades and even centuries old, can redefine their curriculum to meet today's challenges and demands, so can a public school redefine its classroom.

Critical about Special Education

Without a doubt, as a doctoral student, I have become critical of education; especially, I am critical of special education. Even though I look with enthusiasm at the new wave of social literature in special education (Danforth & Gabel, 2006; Erevelles, 2005; Gabel & Peters, 2004; Reiser, 2006a), fostering a consciousness for social justice for the disabled, I am still puzzled as to what it is that we are striving for in the education of special needs students. I find it very problematic that only until recently disability scholars started to question the hegemonic power arrangements of standardization in special education (Erevelles, 2006; Rice, 2006), when these are questions that have been proposed for quite some time in the rest of the educational field (Aoki, 1989/1990; Apple, 1993; Chomsky & Macedo, 2000; Counts, 1932; Dewey, 1916/1944; Freire, 1970; Kozol, 1992; McLaren, 1980).

I do not deny that there are many academics, teachers, advocates, and facilitators out there wondering how to best educate the disabled.

However, I do not see a moral debate of special education at any great length. Like the rest of public education, I have witnessed failed attempts to reform the program without success. At the heart of the problem, what I see happening is not a cultural and social redefinition of the field (Purpel, 1989), nor do I see that special education has changed much from the days that I was receiving the services as a student. If anything, the latest waves of reforms in special education only put more legal strains and demands on teachers and administrators. This leaves me with two thoughts, especially after attending an education conference recently in Austin, Texas, where I observed and participated in some sessions on special education. First, I still wonder why we have become silent about a moral debate in special education. Secondly, I am still puzzled as to why we are accepting such low standards of education, which also includes special education.

As I said, I never became an architect. This, however, does not mean that I never learned anything from my experience in architecture schools. We never attended regular lectures, except for the obvious core courses. We were allowed to work at our own pace. Often, we gathered with the professors in round-table sessions. Studios were physically open without walls. We had no schedules. In many ways, I am reminded of the days when I was in primary school. I cannot help but make a comparison between my experiences in architecture and public schools.

At some point, it has become acceptable to implement a rigid bell-to-bell schedule in schools where discipline is enforced and attention to the teacher is demanded. On top of that, teachers are expected to teach anywhere from 24 to 32 hours a week, giving them very little time for lesson planning. On top of that, teachers are also bound to follow their own set rules and regulations, which, more often than not, would be totally unacceptable and not tolerated in any other working environment. Again, I find it troublesome that only recently scholars in disability studies are daring to discuss the unbendable disciplinary nature of public schools in relation to special education (Erevelles, 2006; Rice, 2006).

As I mentioned before, there is very little argument in society about the goal of education (Purpel, 1989). We may disagree about how to educate the students, what body of knowledge we should transmit, and what values we may inculcate; however, we do not tend to quarrel about the basic assumptions of public education (R. Miller, 1990/1997). We expect public schools to help our students to become model citizens and productive members of society. We expect our teachers to be role models and mold our children into their example. Nevertheless, society has become silent when it comes to providing schools and teachers with very little in terms of resources. To this day, I am still wondering why this is not questioned, especially in an industrialized nation where billions of dollars are wasted somewhere else.

I took this challenge because of the lack of serious moral questioning of the field of special education, but most importantly because of our societal attitude as a whole. I was originally hired to teach resource social studies and math, and my duty was to make them good and productive citizens. However, I was repeatedly told to be realistic about my students, and that I should not expect much from them. One day in class, I said that I find schools to be prisons. My students were originally shocked by my remarks, but they agreed with me, as the conversation progressed. This made me wonder about the true purpose of education.

On the eve of a serious worldwide financial debacle, the resurgence of the cold war, the spread of a new wave of famine in Africa, the serious threat of nuclear terrorism, and the world inaction to stand against new atrocious acts of genocide, I see very little happening in the schools to awaken our students to these tremendous challenges and realities. These are definitely challenges that will affect their lives in multiple forms for many years to come.

When I propose the question in my schools as to why this is not happening, I get a shrug from colleagues, as if these are not topics relevant to a school setting. If that is the case, then, I wonder why we have not demanded a curriculum that will prepare our students to meet such challenges; furthermore, I wonder why we have stood silently, accepting such a low standard of education, where teachers themselves do not expect much from their own students.

I am not claiming to be different. As a teacher in the trenches, I am also part of the army of educators who strive everyday to provide the best for our students and who are consumed by the daily demands. Such demands also have an impact on me, as I can go an entire day in my work without critically thinking about what I am doing and how I am preparing my students for these monumental challenges. However, as a doctoral student, I have become more critical of the special education field. The current dichotomy that exists between regular education and special education deeply troubles me—as if those who are able and those who are disabled exist in two different worlds. We can have countless answers as to why this is happening. Nevertheless, my main concern is that this speaks volumes about our current unwillingness to visualize a more humane and liberating pedagogy for the disabled. This is also true for mainstream students. I am left with the belief that something is fundamentally flawed in the educational discourse and in the system.

My project and the questions which I have proposed have been met with a dual response. On the one hand, such questions have not been very well received in the public education setting; on the contrary, colleagues in the public schools have expressed their sarcasm and disbelief, indicating that there is a real world of the trenches, which is different from the academic world. On the other hand, the academic world has received such questions with open arms, fully acknowledging that there is an urgent need to address such topics. For years, I have been critical of the disconnection between the academic world and the "real" trenches of public school. Although I am still not sure as to why this is happening, I do know there is an adamant resistance to change in public education. As a teacher, I see it everyday.

I need to admit that I am also part of the profession. While I am critical of special education, I have often fallen victim to what the public education does to the average teacher. I have also become sarcastic about the notion that nothing changes, that things are as they are, and that I need to go with the flow, especially after a frustrating day at work. I have never felt good about admitting this; it only comes after years of self-reflection about myself. If anything, by becoming critical about general and special education, I have to become honest about my limitations, boundaries, and nuances of my persona.

I am not sure if I can get past my limitations 100 percent, as I am not equally sure that any educator can. I do know that getting past limitations involves a critical look at one's self-identity, which prepares one for the moral imperatives of educating the disabled. I want to believe that this opportunity allows me to position myself in a better place for what it means to become an educator for the disabled. I hope that what I have to say resonates well with those working alongside with me in the trenches, with those on the cusp of entering special education, and with those involved in other areas of education.

My Goal

From the beginning, my goal in this project has been to propose a better understanding of special education and general education. This has not come easily; nevertheless, it has also yielded a great transformation within me. By welcoming such complexities and challenges, I firmly envision engaging young minds.

Should teachers become engaged in a transformation from mere dispensers of scripted knowledge to educators facilitating knowledge production, I can only hope that they will maintain their enthusiasm for the challenges and complexities that such undertaking represents. This will require a certain amount of honesty, which at times I believe that I do not posses. It will challenge us to be honest about special education, our practice, and it will require us to take an honest look at our attitude towards the profession and the disabled. It will challenge the teacher to be honest about the dominant hegemonic forces of public schools, which demand the implementation of cookbook recipes and cures into the practice. The teacher, undertaking such transformation, must become an advocate, especially for those in greater need.

My task is not easy, as I said before. It has not been easy to look at my life as a disabled. It requires me to be honest about what it means to be a disabled in my life, which I have not done before. Like any other disabled, I have questions, doubts, and anxieties about my reality. It has also required me to display a significant amount of openness about my private life, which was not easy. However, I do not believe that this can be done in any other way. If anything, I take this opportunity to position myself as an advocate for a more honest form of education, where teaching becomes an art and not the mere dispensing of knowledge.

Parting Words

During my junior year in college, for an entire week, I worked and camped in the school around the clock, with very little sleep. I finished my final model late the night before grading. The next day, my professor, barely disguising her dislike for the model, started to pull it apart. "This is not a finished model. No model is ever finished," she said before walking away. Like that architecture model, this is not a finished project either.

I certainly expect those who read this project to do it with criticism, skepticism, and even disagreement. I expect my findings to be questioned, my arguments to be found insufficient, and my reasoning to be challenged. I do expect people to pull apart this model, which has taken me years to build, as my professor pulled apart the model that took me four days of nonstop-sleepless work to complete. I expect flaws to be found. Such actions are legitimate and required, for the sake of advancing our hope for a more humane education for all students. What I ask from the readers, however, is that they not only pinpoint my faults and shortcomings—this surely must be done—but that they also address the need to affirm this kind of work and the particular visions that I provide.

This is welcomed because my most fervent hope is that this project will stimulate others to reflect and engage in clarifying their convictions for envisioning a more humane pedagogy for the disabled. My challenge, for those who read this work, is that they confront the questions of what it is that we are working so hard to make happen. If my convictions are unclear, in what ways ought they be clarified? If my arguments are insufficient, what should be deleted or added? If my creedal statements are problematic, what should we say about developing a better criteria for judging and evaluating special education socially, politically, culturally, and most importantly, spiritually? I certainly look forward to this dialogue.

Like I said before, it was never my intention to unveil a version of what to do in the field of special education. I never sought to provide a new special formula of what to do. I am the first to acknowledge my imperfections as a teacher, and I am the first to state that there are far more competent and better teachers than myself. My goal was, from the beginning, to acknowledge the need for a moral debate in special education. In that regard, I believe I am faithful to my commitment to critical and moral pedagogy—theories that are true to the evolutionary social nature of education (Valentine, 2007). As I finish these lines, I hope that I can transgress beyond the rigid implementation of structures and blueprints, but seek an inner spiritual transformation of the self.

As I conclude this work, memories of the past and the recent present come to my mind. I have memories of my early years, when I truly enjoyed my educational experience, encountering teachers who impacted my life for many years. I also have recent memories of current colleagues, whom I admire, silently watching how dedicated they are to their profession. Memories of my own experience as a special education student resurface, an experience in which I was never happy, but I was never able to understand why. I also have fond memories of my life in the doctoral cohort, where I believe that my life, as a human being, was forever transformed.

Earlier, I said that I do not know exactly why I became a teacher. However, I believe I became a teacher because I love the school setting with its pulsating beat of the bell and classes, students, hallways, bands, athletics, arts, science, and humanities—all encapsulated in a building, where no single day is similar to the next.

Other than proposing what needs to happen in special education, I would pose that it is indeed difficult to point out exactly what needs to occur. Special education is frustrating, yet it can be rewarding. Special education can be neurotic, yet it will not bring you to the breaking point. Special education is energetic, yet it can be lousy. Special education is unique and the disabled students are unique, yet education is unique and every student is unique. It is for this matter that I chose to look at my life as a teacher and a disabled. In these lines, I have attempted to address the need for a moral and ethical discourse in special education. I talked about my life as an immigrant, disabled, avid world traveler, teacher, and doctoral student. Part of this project is to keep it real. It is the only way to seek enlightenment, empowering myself to understand the system while lighting the candle for change.

REFERENCES

Abberley, P. (1987). The concept of oppression and the development of a social theory of disability. *Disability, Handicap & Society, 2*(1), 5–19.

Anyon, J. (2005). *Radical possibilities: Public policy, urban education, and a new social movement.* New York: Routledge.

Aoki, T. (1977). Theoretic dimensions of curriculum: Reflections from a micro-perspective. *Canadian Journal of Education, 2*(1), 49–56.

Aoki, T. (1983). Experiencing ethnicity as a Japanese Canadian teacher: Reflections on a personal curriculum. *Curriculum Inquiry, 13*(3), 321–335.

Aoki, T. (1989/1990). Beyond the half-life of curriculum and pedagogy. *One World, 27*(2), 3–10.

Apple, M. W. (1993). *Official knowledge.* New York: Routledge.

Apple, M. W. (1995). *Education and power* (2nd ed.). New York: Routledge.

Apple, M. W. (2001). Creating profits by creating failures: standards, markets, and inequality in education. *Inclusion Education, 5*(2/3), 103–118.

Apple, M. W. (2005). Are markets in education democratic? Neoliberal globalism, vouchers, and the politics of choice. In M. W. Apple, J. Kenway & M. Singh (Eds.), *Globalizing education: Policies, pedagogies, & politics* (pp. 209–230). New York: Peter Lang.

Apple, M. W., Kenway, J., & Singh, M. (Eds.). (2005). *Globalizing education: Policies, pedagogies, & politics.* New York: Peter Lang.

Asch, A. (2001). Critical race theory, feminism, and disability: Reflections on social justice and personal identity. *Ohio State Law Journal, 62*, 1–17.

Baglieri, S., & Knopf, J. (2004). Normalizing differences in inclusive teaching. *Journal of Learning Disabilities, 37*(6), 525–529.

Barnatt, S., & Scotch, R. (2001). *Disability protest: Contentious politics 1970–1999*. Washington DC: Gallaudet University Press.

Barnes, C. (2003). What a difference a decade makes: Reflection on doing "emancipatory" disability research. *Disability & Society, 18*(1), 3–17.

Barton, L. (1993). An open letter to the powers that be. *Disability, Handicap & Society, 8*(3), 317–327.

Baylies, C. (2002). Disability and the notion of human development: Questions of rights and capabilities. *Disability & Society, 17*(7), 725–739.

Bell, L. A., Washington, S., Weinstein, G., & Love, B. (2003). Knowing ourselves as instructors. In A. Darder, M. Baltodano & R. Torres (Eds.), *The critical pedagogy reader* (pp. 464–478). New York: Routledge-Falmer.

Berliner, D. C., & Biddle, B. J. (1995). *The manufactured crisis: Myths, fraud, and the attack on American public schools*. Cambridge, MA: Perseus Books.

Bissinger, H. G. (2004). *Friday night lights: A town, a team, and a dream*. Cambridge, MA: Da Capo Press.

Blanchet, W. J., Brantlinger, E., & Shealey, M. W. (2005). *Brown* 50 years later—exclusion, segregation and inclusion. *Remedial & Special Education, 26*(2), 66–69.

Blomgren, R. (1998). Special education and the quest for human dignity In H. S. Shapiro & D. E. Purpel (Eds.), *Critical issues in American education: Transformation in a postmodern world* (pp. 241–260). Mahwah, NJ: Lawrence Erlbaum Associates, Publishers.

Britzman, D. P. (2003). *Practice makes practice: A critical study of learning to teach* (Rev. ed.). Albany: State University of New York Press.

Bruner, J. (1990). *Acts of meaning*. Cambridge, MA and London, England: Harvard University Press.

Bruner, J. (1991). The narrative construction of reality. *Critical Inquiry, 18*(1), 1–21.

Bruner, J. (1993). Introduction: The ethnographic self and the personal self. In P. Benson (Ed.), *Anthropology and literature.* Urbana: University of Illinois Press.

Bruner, J. (1996). *The culture of education.* Cambridge, MA: Harvard University Press.

Burch, S., & Sutherland, I. (2006). Who's not here yet? American disability history. *Radical History Review* (94), 127–147.

Burchardt, T. (2004). Capabilities and disabilities: Capabilities framework and the social model of disability. *Disability & Society, 19*(7), 735–751.

Butler, J. (1993). *Bodies that matter: On the discursive limits of sex.* New York: Routledge.

Carr, D. (1986). *Time, narrative, and history.* Bloomington: Indiana University Press.

Carr, M. (1995). A mother's thought on inclusion. In J. Kauffman & D. Hallahan (Eds.), *The illusion of full inclusion: A comprehensive critique of the special education bandwagon* (pp. 263–267). Austin, TX: Pro-Ed.

Chan, E. (2006). Teacher experience of culture in the curriculum. *Journal of Curriculum Studies, 38*(2), 161–176.

Chomsky, N., & Macedo, D. (2000). *Chomsky on miseducation.* Lanham, MD: Rowman & Littlefield Pub.

Clandinin, D. J., & Connelly, F. M. (1992). Teacher as curriculum maker. In P. W. Jackson (Ed.), *Handbook of curriculum* (pp. 363–401). New York: Teacher College Press.

Clandinin, D. J., & Connelly, F. M. (1994). Personal experience method. In N. K. Denzing & Y. S. Lincoln (Eds.), *Handbook of qualitative reasearch* (pp. 413–427). London: Sage Publications.

Clandinin, D. J., & Connelly, F. M. (1995). *Teacher's professional knowledge landscapes.* New York, NY: Teachers College Press.

Clandinin, D. J., & Connelly, F. M. (1996). Teacher's professional knowledge landscape: Teacher stories—stories of teachers—school stories—stories of school. *Educational Researcher, 19*(5), 2–14.

Clandinin, D. J., & Raymond, H. (2006). Note on narrating disability. *Equity & Excellence in Education, 39*(2), 101–114.

Clare, E. (2001). Stolen bodies, reclaimed bodies: Disability and queerness. *Public Culture, 13*(3), 359–365.

Conle, C. (1999). Why narrative? Which narrative? Struggling with time and place in life and research. *Curriculum Inquiry, 29*(7), 7–32.

Conle, C. (2000). Narrative inquiry: Research tool and medium for professional development. *European Journal of Teacher Education, 29*(3), 49–63.

Conle, C. (2001). The rationality of narrative inquiry in research and professional development. *European Journal of Teacher Education, 24*(1), 21–33.

Connelly, F. M., & Clandinin, D. J. (1988). *Teachers as curriculum planners: Narratives of experience.* New York: Teachers College Press.

Connelly, F. M., & Clandinin, D. J. (1990). Stories of experience and narrative inquiry. *Educational Researcher, 19*(5), 2–14.

Connelly, F. M., & Clandinin, D. J. (Eds.). (1999). *Shaping a professional identity: Stories of educational practice.* New York: Teachers College Press.

Connelly, F. M., Clandinin, D. J., & He, M. F. (1997). Teacher's personal practical knowledge on the professional knowledge landscape. *Teaching and Teachers Education, 13*(7), 665–674.

Connelly, F. M., Phillion, J., & He, M. F. (2003). An exploration of narrative inquiry into multiculturalism in education: Reflecting on two decades of research in an inner-city Canadian community school. *Curriculum Inquiry, 33*(4), 363–384.

Counts, G. (1932). *Dare the school build a new social order?* New York: Day.

Counts, G. (1949). The end of a myth about education and democracy. *Vital Speeches of the Day, 15*(9), 266–269.

Covey, H. (1998). *Social perceptions of people with disabilities in history*. Springfields, IL: Charles C. Thomas Publishers.

Craig, C. J. (1995). Crossing the boundaries of the professional knowledge. In F. M. Connelly & D. J. Clandinin (Eds.), *Teachers' professional knowledge landscapes* (pp. 16–24). New York: Teachers College Press.

Craig, C. J. (2000). Stories of school/teacher stories: A two-part invention on the walls theme. *Curriculum Inquiry, 30*(1), 11–41.

Craig, C. J. (2001). The relationship between and among teachers' narrative knowledge, communities of knowing, and school reform: A case of "the Monkey's Paw." *Curriculum Inquiry, 31*(3), 303–331.

Craig, C. J. (2003). Story constellations. *Curriculum & Teaching Dialogue, 5*(1), 31–41.

Craig, C. J. (2006a). Musings on the margin. *Curriculum & Teaching Dialogue, 8*(1/2), 3–14.

Craig, C. J. (2006b). Why is dissemination so difficult? The nature of teacher knowledge and the spread of curriculum reform. *American Educational Research Journal, 43*(2), 257–293.

Cremin, L. (1983). The problematics of education in the 1980s: Some reflections on the Oxford workshop. *Oxford Review of Education, 8*(1), 9–20.

Crites, S. (1971). The narrative quality of experience. *Journal of the American Academy of Religion, 39*(3), 291–311.

Danermark, B., & Gellerstedt, L. C. (2004). Social justice: Redistribution and recognition—a non-reductionist perspective on disability. *Disability & Society, 19*(4), 339–353.

Danforth, S., & Gabel, S. L. (Eds.). (2006). *Vital questions facing disability studies in education*. New York: Peter Lang Publishing.

Darder, A., Baltodano, M., & Torres, R. (Eds.). (2003). *The critical pedagogy reader*. New York: Routledge-Falmer.

Dewey, J. (1897). My pedagogic creed. *School Journal, 54*, 77–80.

Dewey, J. (1908/1981). The practical character of reality. In J. McDermott (Ed.), *The philosophy of John Dewey*. Chicago, IL: University of Chicago Press (Originally published in 1908).

Dewey, J. (1916/1944). *Democracy and education: An introduction to philosophy of education*. New York: Free Press (Original work published in 1916).

Dewey, J. (1934). *Art as experience*. New York: Berkley Publishing Group.

Dewey, J. (1938a). *Experience and education*. New York: Macmillan.

Dewey, J. (1938b). *Logic: The theory of Inquiry*. New York: Henry Holt and Company.

Dewey, J. (1944). *Democracy and education: An introduction to philosophy of education*. New York: Free Press (Original work published in 1916).

Edgar, E. (1997). School reform, special education, and democracy. *Remedial & Special Education, 18*(6), 323–325.

Eisner, E. (2001). What does it mean to say a school is doing well? *Phi Delta Kappan, 82*(5), 367–372.

Eisner, E. (2002). The kind of schools we need. *Phi Delta Kappan, 83*(8), 576–583.

Eisner, E. (2005). Back to whole. *Educational Leadership, 63*(1), 14–18.

Eisner, E. (2006). The satisfaction of teaching. *Educational Leadership, 63*(6), 44–46.

Ellis, C. (1997). Evocative autoethnography: Writing emotionally about our lives. In W. G. Tierney & Y. S. Lincoln (Eds.), *Representation and text: Reframing the narrative voice* (pp. 115–139). Albany: State University of New York.

Ellis, C. (2002). Being real: Moving inward toward social change. *Qualitative Studies in Education, 15*(4), 399–406.

Ellis, C. (2004). *The ethnographic I: A methodological novel about autoethnography*. Walnut Creek, CA: AltaMira Press.

Emery, K. (2002). *The business roundtable and systemic reform: How corporate-engineered high-stakes testing has eliminated community participation in developing educational goals and policies*. University of California, Davis.

Erevelles, N. (2000). Educating unruly bodies: Critical pedagogy, disability studies and the politics of schooling. *Education Theory, 50*(1), 25–48.

Erevelles, N. (2002). (Im)material citizens: Cognitive disability, race and the politics of citizenship. *Disability, Culture and Education, 1*(1), 5–25.

Erevelles, N. (2005). Understanding curriculum as a normalized text: Disability studies meet curriculum theory. *Journal of Curriculum Studies, 37*(4), 421–439.

Erevelles, N. (2006). Deconstructing difference: Doing disability studies in multicultural educational context. In S. Danforth & S. L. Gabel (Eds.), *Vital questions facing disability studies in education* (pp. 363–378). New York: Peter Lang Publishing.

Ferri, B., & Connor, D. (2005). Tools of exclusion: Race, disability and (re)segregated education. *Teachers College Record, 107*(3), 453–474.

Freire, P. (1970). *Pedagogy of the oppressed*. New York: Herder and Herder.

Freire, P. (1970/2000). *Pedagogy of the oppressed*. New York: Continuum (original work published in 1970).

Freire, P. (2000). *Pedagogy of the oppressed*. New York: Continuum.

Fulton, S. A., & Sabornie, E. J. (1994). Evidence of employment inequality among females with disabilities. *Journal of Special Education, 28*(2), 149–167.

Gabel, S. (2002). Some conceptual problems with critical pedagogy. *Curriculum Inquiry, 32*(2), 177–201.

Gabel, S., & Peters, S. (2004). Presage of paradigm shift? Beyond the social model of disability toward resistance theories of disability. *Disability & Society, 19*(6), 585–600.

Gallagher, J. J. (1995). The pull of societal forces on special education. In J. Kauffman & D. Hallahan (Eds.), *The illusion of full inclusion: A comprehensive critique of the special education bandwagon* (pp. 91–103). Austin, TX: Pro-Ed.

Gilbert, T., Cochrane, A., & Greenwell, S. (2005). Citizenship: Locating people with learning disabilities. *International Journal of Social Welfare, 14*(4), 287–296.

Giroux, H. (1988). *Teachers as intellectuals: Towards a critical pedagogy of learning*. Hadley, MA: Bergin & Garvey.

Giroux, H. (2003a). Education incorporated? In A. Darder, M. Baltodano & R. Torres (Eds.), *The critical pedagogy reader* (pp. 119–125). New York: Routledge-Falmer.

Giroux, H. (2003b). Towards a postmodern pedagogy. In L. Cahoone (Ed.), *From modernism to postmodernism: An Anthology*. Oxford, England: Blackwell Publishing.

Gore, J. (2003). What can we do for you! What *can* "we" do for "you": Struggling over empowerment in critical and femenist pedagogy. In A. Darder, M. Baltodano & R. Torres (Eds.), *The critical pedagogy reader* (pp. 331–348). New York: Routledge-Falmer.

Greene, M. (2003). In search of critical pedagogy. In A. Darder, M. Baltodano & R. Torres (Eds.), *The critical pedagogy reader* (pp. 97–112). New York: Routledge-Falmer.

Hamilton, M. L. (1996). *Mapping a terrain: Identifying and exploring self-study*. Paper presented at the American Education Research Association, New York.

Handley, P. (2003). Theorising disability: Beyond "common sense." *Politics, 23*(2), 109–118.

Hansen, D. T. (1998). The importance of the person in the role of teacher. *Child & Adolescent Social Work Journal, 15*(5), 391–405.

Hansen, D. T. (2004). A poetics of teaching. *Educational Theory, 54*(2), 119–142.

Haraway, D. (1990). A manifesto for Cyborgs: Science, technology, and social feminism in the 1980's. In L. Nicholson (Ed.), *Feminism/Postmodernism* (pp. 190–233). New York: Routledge.

Hatt, B. (2005). Pedagogical love in the transactional curriculum. *Journal of Curriculum Studies, 37*(6), 671–688.

Hehir, T. (2005). *New directions in special education: Eliminating ableism in policy and practice.* Cambridge, MA: Harvard Education Press.

Ho, A. (2004). To be labelled, or not to be labelled: That is the question. *British Journal of Learning Disabilities, 32*, 86–92.

Howe, K., & Miramontes, O. (1991). A framework for ethical deliberation of special education. *Journal of Special Education, 25*(1), 7–25.

Hursh, D. (2006). The crisis in urban education: Resisting neoliberal policies and forging democratic possibilities. *Educational Researcher, 35*(4), 19–25.

Kauffman, J., & Hallahan, D. (Eds.). (1995). *The illusion of full inclusion: A comprehensive critique of a current special education bandwagon.* Austin, TX: Pro-Ed.

Kincheloe, J. L. (1997). Fiction formulas: Critical constructivism and the representation of reality. In W. G. Tierney & Y. S. Lincoln (Eds.), *Representation and text: Reframing the narrative voice* (pp. 57–80). Albany: State University of New York.

Kincheloe, J. L. (2002). *Getting beyond the facts: Teaching social studies/social sciences in the twenty-first century* (2nd ed.). New York: Peter Lang.

Kincheloe, J. L. (2004). *Critical pedagogy primer.* New York: Peter Lang.

Kincheloe, J. L. (2007). Critical pedagogy in the twenty-first century: Evolution for survival. In P. McLaren & J. L. Kincheloe (Eds.), *Critical pedagogy: Where are we now?* (pp. 9–42). New York: Peter Lang Publishing.

Kozol, J. (1992). *Savage inequalities: Children in America's schools.* New York: Harper Perennial.

Kozol, J. (2005). *The shame of the nation: The restoration of apartheid schooling in America.* New York: Crown Publishers.

Liss, N. (2003). What we talk about when we talk about social studies. *Social Studies, 94*(6), 245–251.

Loewen, J. W. (1995). *Lies my teacher told me: Everything your American history textbook got wrong*. New York: Norton.

Longmore, P. (1995). Medical decision making and people with disabilities: A clash of cultures. *Journal of Law, Medicine & Ethics, 23*(1), 82–87.

Mariage, T. V., Paxton-Buursma, D. J., & Bouck, E. C. (2004). Interanimation: Repositioning possibilities in educational context. *Journal of Learning Disabilities, 37*(6), 534–549.

Matthiessen, P. (1978). *The snow leopard*. New York: Penguin.

McLaren, P. (1980). *Cries from the corridor*. Toronto; New York: Methuen.

McLaren, P. (1997). The ethnographer as a postmodern flâneur: Critical reflexivity and posthybridity as narrative engagement. In W. G. Tierney & Y. S. Lincoln (Eds.), *Representation and text: Reframing the narrative voice* (pp. 144–177). Albany: State University of New York.

McLaren, P. (2003a). Critical pedagogy: A look at the major concepts. In A. Darder, M. Baltodano & R. Torres (Eds.), *The critical pedagogy reader* (pp. 69–96). New York: Routledge-Falmer.

McLaren, P. (2003b). *Life in schools: An introduction to critical pedagogy in the foundations of education*. Boston: Allyn and Bacon.

McLaren, P. (2003c). Revolutionary pedagogy in post-revolutionary times. In A. Darder, M. Baltodano & R. Torres (Eds.), *The critical pedagogy reader* (pp. 151–184). New York: Routledge-Falmer.

McLaren, P., & Farahmandpur, R. (2005). *Teaching against global capitalism and the new imperialism: A critical pedagogy*. Lanham, MD: Rowman & Littlefield.

McNiff, J. (2007, July 2, 2007). *The significance of "I" in educational research and the responsibility of intellectuals*. Paper presented at the New Horizons for Quality in Higher Education and Training, Pretoria, South Africa.

Miller, J. L. (1982). The sound of silence breaking: Feminist pedagogy and curriculum theory. *JTC, 4*(1), 5–11.

Miller, J. L. (1990). *Creating spaces and finding voices: Teachers collaborating for empowerment*. Albany: State University of New York Press.

Miller, R. (1990/1997). *What schools are for: Holistic education in American culture.* Brandon, VT: Holistic Education Press (Originally published in 1990).

Miller, R. (1997). *What schools are for: Holistic education in American culture.* Brandon, VT: Holistic Education Press.

Miller, S. R. (1981). A crisis in appropriate education: The dearth of data on programs for secondary handicapped adolescent *The Journal of Special Education, 15*(3), 351–360.

Mitra, S. (2006). The capabilty approach and disability. *Journal of Disability Policy Studies, 16*(4), 236–247.

Moen, T. (2006). Reflections on the narrative research approach. *International Journal of Qualitative Methods, 5*(4), 1–11.

Mouffe, C. (1996). Radical democracy or liberal democracy. In D. Trend (Ed.), *Radical Democracy* (pp. 19–26). New York: Routledge.

Muncey, T. (2005). Doing autoethnography. *International Journal of Qualitative Methods, 4*(1), 1–12.

Oliver, M. (1986). Social policy and disability: Some theoretical issues. *Disability, Handicap & Society, 1*(1), 5–17.

Oliver, M. (1992). Changing the social relations of research productions? *Disability, Handicap & Society, 7*(2), 101–114.

Oliver, M., & Zarb, G. (1989). The politics of disability: A new approach. *Disability, Handicap & Society, 4*(3), 221–239.

Olson, M. R., & Craig, C. J. (2005). Uncovering cover stories: Tensions and entailments in the development of teacher knowledge. *Curriculum Inquiry, 35*(2), 161–182.

Osgood, R. (2005). *The history of inclusion in the United States.* Washington DC : Gaulladet University Press.

Paul, J., French, P., & Cramston-Gingras, A. (2001). Ethics and Special Education. *Focus on special education, 34*(1), 1–16.

Pinar, W. F. (1997). Regimes of reason and the male narrative voice. In W. G. Tierney & Y. S. Lincoln (Eds.), *Representation and text: Reframing the narrative voice* (pp. 81–113). Albany: State University of New York Press.

Polanyi, M. (1961). Knowing and being. *Mind, 70*(280), 458–470.

Polanyi, M. (1966). The logic of tacit interference. *Philosophy, 41*(155), 1–18.

Polkinghorne, D. E. (1997). Reporting qualitative research as practice. In W. G. Tierney & Y. S. Lincoln (Eds.), *Representation and text: Reframing the narrative voice* (pp. 3–21). Albany: State University of New York Press.

Purpel, D. E. (1989). *The moral & spiritual crisis in education: A curriculum for justice and compassion in education.* Granby, MS: Bergin & Garvey Publishers.

Purpel, D. E. (2003). The decontextualization of moral education. *American Journal of Education, 110*, 89–95.

Purpel, D. E., & McLaurin, W. M. (2004). *Reflections on the moral and spiritual crisis in education.* New York: Peter Lang.

Rawls, J. (1971). *A theory of justice.* Cambridge, MA: Belknap Press of Harvard University Press.

Reiser, R. (2006a). Disability equality: Confronting the oppression of the past. In M. Cole (Ed.), *Education, equality and human rights: Issues of gender, "race," sexuality, disability, and social class* (pp. 134–179). London/New York: Routledge.

Reiser, R. (2006b). Inclusive education or special educational needs: meeting the challenge of disability discrimination in schools. In M. Cole (Ed.), *Education, equality and human rights: Issues of gender, "race," sexuality, disability, and social class* (pp. 157–179). London/New York: Routledge.

Rice, N. (2006). Teacher education as a site of resistance. In S. Danforth & S. L. Gabel (Eds.), *Vital questions facing disability studies in education* (pp. 17–32). New York: Peter Lang Publishing.

Rose, C. (1997). Shaping Sara's practice. In W. G. Tierney & Y. S. Lincoln (Eds.), *Representation and text: Reframing the narrative voice* (pp. 42–63). Albany: State University of New York Press.

Ross, V. (2003). Walking around the curriculum tree: An analysis of a third/fourth-grade mathematics lesson. *Journal of Curriculum Studies, 35*(5), 567–584.

Russell, M. (1998). *Beyond ramps: Disability at the end of the social contract: A warning from an Uppity Crip*. Monroe, ME: Common Courage Press.

Schön, D. A. (1991). *The reflective practioner: Case studies in and on educational practice*. New York: Basic Books.

Schön, D. A., & Rein, M. (1994). *Frame reflection: Toward the resolution of intractable policy controversies*. New York: BasicBooks.

Schwab, J. (1960). What do scientists do? *Behavioral Science, 5*(1), 1–27.

Schwab, J. (1971). The practical: Arts of eclectic. *The School Review, 79*(4), 493–452.

Schwab, J. (1973). The practical 3: Translation into curriculum. *The School Review, 79*(4), 493–542.

Seaman, M. L. (2006). *First-year teacher, second time around: A narrative self-study of teaching in higher education*. University of Houston, Houston, Texas: Unpublished doctoral dissertation.

Seaman, M. L. (2008). *First-year teacher, second time around: An autobiographical self-study of teaching in higher education*. Saarbrücken, Germany: VMD Verlag.

Shapiro, H. S. (1998). Clinton and education: Policies without meaning. In H. S. Shapiro & D. E. Purpel (Eds.), *Critical issues in American education: Transformation in a postmodern world* (pp. 45–55). Mahwah, NJ: Lawrence Erlbaum Associates, Publishers.

Shapiro, J. (1998). The American with minor disabilities act. *U. S. News & World Report, 125,* 41–42.

Singh, M., Kenway, J., & Apple, M. W. (2005). Globalizing education: Perspectives from above and below. In M. W. Apple, J. Kenway & M. Singh (Eds.), *Globalizing education: Policies, pedagogies, & politics* (pp. 1–29). New York: Peter Lang.

Skrtic, T. M. (1995). The crisis in professional knowledge. In E. I. Meyen & T. M. Skrtic (Eds.), *Special education and student disability: An introduction* (4th ed.). Denver, CO: Love.

Stiker, H. (1999). *A history of disability* (W. Sayers, Trans.). Ann Arbor: University of Michigan Press.

Talbert, T. (2002). McFreedom? Packaging democracy for students consumption. *Simile, 2*(1).

Tierney, W. G. (2002). Writing matters. *International Journal of Qualitative Studies in Education, 14*(4), 427–430.

Tierney, W. G., & Lincoln, Y. S. (Eds.). (1997). *Representation and text: Reframing the narrative voice.* Albany: State University of New York Press.

Tregaskis, C. (2004). Applying the social model in practice: some lessons from countryside recreation. *Disability & Society, 19*(6), 601–611.

Urban, W. J., & Wagoner, J. L. (2000). *American education: A history* (2nd ed.). Boston: McGraw-Hill.

Valentine, J. (2007). How can we transgress in the field of disabilities in urban education? In S. R. Steinberg & J. L. Kincheloe (Eds.), *19 urban questions: Teaching in the city* (pp. 127–142). New York: Peter Lang.

Whelan, K. (1997). Traveler on a journey. In W. G. Tierney & Y. S. Lincoln (Eds.), *Representation and text: Reframing the narrative voice* (pp. 20–31). Albany, NY: State University of New York Press.

White, C., Liss, N., & Marsh, S. (2007). *"Urban" education issues: Educator conversations.* Paper presented at the American Education Research Association, Chicago, IL.

White, C., & McCormack, S. (2006). The message in the music: Popular culture and teaching social studies. *Social Studies, 93*(3), 122–127.

Zinn, H. (2003). *A people's history of the United States: 1492-present*. New York: Harper-Collins.

COUNTERPOINTS

Studies in the Postmodern Theory of Education

General Editor
Shirley R. Steinberg

Counterpoints publishes the most compelling and imaginative books being written in education today. Grounded on the theoretical advances in criticalism, feminism, and postmodernism in the last two decades of the twentieth century, Counterpoints engages the meaning of these innovations in various forms of educational expression. Committed to the proposition that theoretical literature should be accessible to a variety of audiences, the series insists that its authors avoid esoteric and jargonistic languages that transform educational scholarship into an elite discourse for the initiated. Scholarly work matters only to the degree it affects consciousness and practice at multiple sites. Counterpoints' editorial policy is based on these principles and the ability of scholars to break new ground, to open new conversations, to go where educators have never gone before.

For additional information about this series or for the submission of manuscripts, please contact:

Shirley R. Steinberg
c/o Peter Lang Publishing, Inc.
29 Broadway, 18th floor
New York, New York 10006

To order other books in this series, please contact our Customer Service Department:

(800) 770-LANG (within the U.S.)
(212) 647-7706 (outside the U.S.)
(212) 647-7707 FAX

Or browse online by series:

www.peterlang.com